CUSH:
A CIVIL WAR
MEMOIR

CUSH:
A CIVIL WAR
MEMOIR

by Samuel H. Sprott

edited by
Louis R. Smith, Jr.
&
Andrew Quist

Livingston Press
at
The University of West Alabama

ISBN 0-942979-55-9, paper
ISBN 0-942979-56-7, hardbound

Library of Congress #99-068022

First edition.

Manufactured in the United States of America.

Printing: Great Plains Printing Company
Hardback Binding: Heckman Bindery

Typing: Lee Gosselin
Typesetting: Lee Gosselin & Jill Wallace
Proofreading: Tina N. Jones, Louis Smith, Andrew Quist, Joe Taylor,
Lee Gosselin, Amanda Snipes, Jill Wallace,
and Stephanie Parnell
Indexing: Amanda Snipes & Jill Wallace

*The Alabama regiment flag on the back was provided courtesy of
http://tennesee-sev.org.*

**Special thanks to the Sumter County Historical Society for
funding this project.**

Table of Contents

continued, next page

PREFACE

In 1963 I read Bell Irvin Wiley's *The Life of Johnny Reb: The Common Soldier of the Confederacy* as part of the requirements for a United States history survey course at Birmingham-Southern College. Until that time both my knowledge and my interest in the Confederacy had centered around the dashing and daring cavalry leaders epitomized by Stuart, Forrest, and Morgan. I found Wiley's work fascinating because the problems and challenges which typical soldiers faced during that conflict had never occurred to me. I majored in history at Birmingham-Southern, but the Civil War was not my focus. Wiley's work became a footnote in my historical studies until I began work on my dissertation at the University of Alabama in 1985.

As a native of Sumter County I was aware of numerous primary sources which were available locally. Armed with that knowledge, I determined that writing a history of Sumter County was a do-able dissertation project. My friend the late Jud Arrington, local historian and preserver of Sumter County history, became my mentor. Soon after beginning my project, I met Jud in the Sumter County Probate Office and he showed me Judge Samuel Sprott's serialized history in the now defunct *Our Southern Home* newspaper. As is often the case with research, I suspended work on the current project long enough to devour Sprott's work.

While reading Sprott, I reflected on Wiley's descriptions that I had read some twenty years earlier. The trials and disparity of life as a soldier which Wiley recounted in general terms came to life as I read Sprott's recounting of the Fortieth Alabama Regiment of Infantry and his unit, the South Sumter Guard. In addition to his personal recollections, Sprott had several journals and diaries from men who had served in his unit. Armed with this wealth of first-hand information, Sprott detailed the military maneuvers of his unit and the Fortieth Alabama, often challenging other contemporary accounts. Interspersed among the military events are what I believe to be the heart of Sprott's memoir—accounts of events and episodes of individuals who were not only soldiers but also men. He recounts the typical soldier's complaints about army food, and softens the telling with his recipe for the Southern staple he called "cush." When the South Sumter Guard were positioned on the Alabama eastern shore they witnessed a "Jubilee" occurring along Mobile Bay. Sprott captures the event with the same scientific explanation that accompanies such an occurrence today. He tells of Federal and Confederate pickets sharing breakfast and trading supplies each morning during a lull in the fighting, and he speaks of meeting a fellow Sumter Countian from another unit who is going home to raise corn for the "cause" because he can't stop his legs from running when the first shots of battle are fired. In addition to the poignant stories that speak to the humanity of war, Sprott's work is also noteworthy because it chronicles much of the history of the Fortieth Alabama, a "run-of-the-mill Confederate unit" about which little has been written.

Following the completion of my dissertation in 1988 and at the urging of Dr. Forrest McDonald and Dr. Gary Mills, I again began to think about the Sprott papers and an appropriate project. I completed the transcription of the papers in 1992 and shared what I had with my cousin, David Neel, an avid student and re-enactor of the Civil War. David suggested that Sprott's accounts, though while substantially accurate, might be enhanced if they were tied to the Official Records of the War Between the States. David worked on that aspect of the project until 1998 when work and family responsibilities forced him to relinquish the task to Andrew Quist, a friend of David's and fellow re-enactor. A history major at the University of West Alabama, Andrew embraced the project and completed his work in the summer of 1999.

The Fortieth Alabama Regiment

It is not unfair to say that the Fortieth Alabama Regiment of Infantry was a run-of-the-mill Confederate unit. The Fortieth Alabama was organized at Demopolis, Alabama, in the Spring of 1862 from companies recruited in west central Alabama. This was the great second wave of Confederate enlistment, and recruits found their way into the command by several paths. Some men had joined earlier and were sent home because of lack of arms and equipment. Others had joined the Alabama State Militia for twelve months of duty and now as their enlistments were expiring reenlisted for three years or the war. Still others were nudged into volunteering before the Conscript Act mandated military service for many Southern men, because they felt confident that those who had to be compelled by force of law to do their duty would be shamed by the folks at home.

After two months of training in Demopolis, the unit was sent to Cantonment Walter at Dog River Factory near Mobile, Alabama, to defend the city. In December, 1862, the troops were shipped to Mississippi and the unit was assigned to various duties and locations. Eventually, the Fortieth Alabama was sent to Vicksburg. Upon its arrival, the unit found Vicksburg invested and Grant's siege of the river port inevitable. The unit was divided, with most of the regiment staying in Vicksburg attached to Brigadier John C. Moore's Brigade of Texas, Alabama, and Mississippi troops and eventually surrendering, and the remainder, which comprised Stone's Battalion, serving on detached duty north of Vicksburg under the command of Major Thomas Oswalt Stone. At the fall of Vicksburg, the Confederates attached Stone's Battalion to General Matthew Duncan Ector's Brigade from Texas. As members of Ector's Brigade, Sprott and the remaining Alabamians were involved in the heavy engagements at Chickamauga and later after reuniting with the Fortieth fought at Missionary Ridge. The reunited regiment was involved in the vigorous action of Moore's Brigade that stemmed the Federal assault on Missionary Ridge on November 25, 1863, solidifying the position of the right wing of General Braxton Bragg's forces and allowing for a timely withdrawal by those troops. After participating in the early stages of the Atlanta Campaign, the regiment was ordered to Mobile with the assignment of bolstering the city's defenses. Following uneventful duty in and around Baldwin County and after the fall of Atlanta, the Fortieth was sent to the Carolinas where it fought in the Battle of Bentonville, one of the last engagements of the War.

Louis R. Smith, Jr. and David S. Neel, Jr.

Judge Samuel Henry Sprott

Samuel H. Sprott was born on June 24, 1840, in Sumter County, Alabama. He was one of six children of Mary (Bothwell) and Robert Sprott, both of whom immigrated to the United States from Ireland in 1838. Within a year they had moved to Alabama and settled on farmland in Sumter County. Sprott attended local schools and completed his education at Barton Academy in Mobile. His family was Scotch-Irish Presbyterian, and he was an active member of this denomination throughout his life.

In the Spring of 1862 Samuel Sprott joined The South Sumter Guards, one of the first companies organized in the county in support of the South's cause in the War Between the States. Sprott enlisted as a private but was quickly elevated to the rank of 3rd Sergeant by his fellow soldiers. The following year Sprott was promoted to Lieutenant. When he surrendered in Salisbury, North Carolina in May 1865, Sprott had attained the rank of Captain of Company A 40th Alabama Regiment.

After the war Sprott taught school and began to study law. In 1867 he was admitted to the bar and began a practice in Livingston, Alabama. Sprott had a number of partners in his practice. Among them were Major Cobbs, W. G. Little, Jr., and J. J. Altman. When Circuit Judge W. S. Mudd resigned in 1883, Governor E. A. O'Neal appointed Sprott to fill Mudd's unexpired term as judge of the sixth judicial circuit of Alabama. When the term expired in 1886, Sprott defeated James B. Head in the general election to remain in office. He served as circuit judge for almost twenty-eight years and retired in 1910. The following year, Sprott was elected to the Alabama Senate where he served for one term.

In 1868 Sprott married Leonora Brockway, the daughter of Dr. A. E. Brockway of Gaston, Alabama. They had six children, two sons and four daughters. For forty years Judge Sprott was an elder in the Livingston Presbyterian Church and was a Royal Arch Mason. Assuming primary responsibility for organizing the Confederate Veterans Association in Sumter County, he was its first Commandant. On April 12, 1916, Judge Sprott died in Jasper, Alabama, at the home of his eldest daughter, Mrs. Augusta Belle Long.

In January, 1899, a series of articles entitled "Sumter in the Civil War" began appearing in *Our Southern Home*, a weekly newspaper published in Livingston, Alabama. Over the next seventeen months Judge Sprott wrote his history of the local units during the war. Sprott used company records, diaries and statements from his fellow soldiers to augment the wealth of first- hand information that was the basis for his articles. In an effort to maintain the factual integrity of his articles, Sprott would ask his readers to report errors to him. When erroneous material was identified, Sprott would verify the corrections and include them in subsequent installments. To our knowledge this material has never been reproduced in printed form.

Although his articles contain some Confederate biases, for the most part they reflect a balanced presentation. He was an accurate observer in relating the major battles in which the men of Sumter's units were engaged, and he was also accurate in recounting their personal stories. The South Sumter Guards served in a variety of locations in at least five states. They saw action in Mobile and Spanish Fort in Alabama; in Vicksburg and northern Mississippi; Chattanooga, Tennessee; Chickamauga and northern Georgia; and North Carolina. Since his unit and others that he discussed served in so many locales, his accounts contain a somewhat universal perspective of the conflict. Judge Sprott's descriptions of the overabundant problems and hardships, plus the rare humorous events that the average soldier encountered, are especially poignant.

Acknowledgements

There are many people to thank. The late Honorable Wilbur Dearman, Probate Judge of Sumter County for over twenty years, preserved the original papers and copies of Sprott's work. My good friend and mentor, Jud Arrington, who knew about Sprott's work, was gracious enough to share that information with me and gently encouraged me as I went about my task. Dr. Joe Taylor and the staff at Livingston Press deserve my gratitude for graciously accepting lame excuses for unwarranted delays. They never gave up on the project or me. Andrew Quist and David Neel contributed many hours of work annotating the chapters and making them more historically sound. The Sumter County Historical Society has been generous on this and many other publishing projects. I am grateful for the enduring faith of my mother Trice Smith. She never wavered in her belief that I would complete the project. My sons, Pat, Jack and Cullen never complained about big events I missed in their lives so I could focus on this event in my life. My wife, Carole, has truly been a partner in this effort. She never gave up on the project or me and without her encouragement, proofreading, and strong admonition that "It's about time to be winding this thing up," I might never have finished it.

Louis R. Smith, Jr.
October 7, 1999

Foreword

I spent the majority of my grade school and high school years reading about the exploits of Robert E. Lee's vaunted Army of Northern Virginia, and I was inspired by a single photograph that many of us have seen. It was taken in the late summer of 1862 and is perhaps the only picture ever taken of Confederate soldiers on the march. The aspect of the photograph that really impressed me was the simplicity of the soldiers. It so happened that the period of time that the photograph was taken was the poorest-equipped period that Lee's army ever experienced. In the picture, the men stand in loose formation during a halt. They are talking to one another and trying to relax during their brief respite. The uniforms they wear are of various types and seem to be in poor repair, reflecting the fact that the Confederate Quartermaster system was not yet operational. Shoeless individuals are also easily spotted. Nonetheless, they stand resolute and full of confidence. A witness to the scene said, " They are a dirty, hungry set of wolves yet there is a dash about them that the northern men lack." The picture corroborates the statement.

Faced with adversity, the men found the courage to continue. They were flush with victory and believed that they and "Bobby" Lee would whip the Yankees on their own soil. It was a crucial time, and they all realized that a crushing Northern defeat could ultimately bring European intervention and their eventual freedom. In short there was hope that Southern independence was at hand. The events that unfolded in the Eastern Theatre have been the most written about military campaigns in American History; as a result, they are what we teach our children in school, and they are really all I knew about the conflict for the first seven years that I studied the war.

That changed for me, however, when I came to The University of West Alabama in the fall of 1993. Once in the "Deep South" I began seeing that the people here did not know as much about Lee as they did an officer named Braxton Bragg. Students of the war didn't talk about "Stonewall" Jackson nearly as much as they did Patrick Cleburne, and "Compared to Nathan Bedford Forrest," they said, "Jeb Stuart was a Boy Scout." Curiosity got the better of me, and I began reading about the relatively obscure fighting in the Western Theatre. As I read, I began to realize that the privations faced by the western Confederate soldier far exceeded those of his eastern counterparts.

Imagine if you will, standing on the edge of a tree line facing an open field. You see the enemy position approximately a mile and a half in front of you. If you were fighting for Robert E. Lee, you would have a far greater advantage than if you were fighting for Braxton Bragg. That advantage was not physical but mental. In Lee's army the men had a much higher level of morale. As soldiers, they believed that their commander would never commit them to an attack that he did not think would result in success. Those in Bragg's army had been bloodied enough to believe that their commander cared little for them. They, in turn, had no faith in him. Yet they would stand and fight with their comrades so that their integrity might be maintained and their homes and families protected.

Confederate Lieutenant General Leonidas Polk once said, "There are some positions in an army where weakness is wickedness." Weak commanders, in key positions plagued the "hard luck" Army of Tennessee. As a result, they had but one major victory over the course of the entire war and little else to inspire them. The stories that these soldiers tell are remarkable. Once in a great while, a new set of memoirs written by a soldier will be uncovered in someone's attic or found buried in obscure town records. These findings shed new light on the War Between the States from the crucial point of view of the common soldier, the man who fought on the line.

Much to my delight, in April of 1998 I was invited to participate in the annotation of such a manuscript that had been retrieved from the county probate records by Louis Smith. The manuscript was written by Judge Samuel H. Sprott and was commenced in January of 1899. The basis of the work is his recollection of the war through the participation of his unit, the 40th Alabama Infantry Regiment. I read the manuscript quickly, gobbling up this fresh and honest insight into the great conflict. I was immediately struck by the lucidity of Sprott's writing and the depth of his descriptions of the life of a common soldier in the Western Theatre. Not knowing half of what I have come to learn of the Western Theatre, I did not pay as much attention to the quality of Sprott's historical content as I did to his descriptions of army life in general and the vivid battle scenes he committed to paper. I found many of Sprott's passages so moving that they produced a lump in my throat. I felt then, as I feel now, that this work is probably one of the most relevant soldier's accounts to come from that tragic time.

My personal basis for such an opinion is borne from a number of factors. The first is the detail of Sprott's descriptions. This is one of the rare memoirs where the author places the reader on the firing line to literally feel the fatigue, thirst, and strain of the battlefield. The only other book that I have read that compares to Sprott's account is Sam Watkin's well known work, *Co. 'Aytch' A Side Show of the Big Show*. Both books serve the reader in presenting an accurate account of the human side of war and how the soldiers lived when they were not in battle. In Sprott's work, the reader learns what the soldiers did to stave off the sheer boredom of camp life. There are louse races, pilfered whiskey rations, and various other light-hearted diversions that only soldiers faced with the deadly reality of war can produce.

Another factor that I came to appreciate is the accuracy of Sprott's historical content. As a history student, I had been taught from my freshman year in college that it is important to view memoirs with a skeptical eye. In many cases, memoirs are written many years after the events that they attempt to describe. The impact of the distance of time often becomes apparent when the authors are caught embellishing memories or simply not being able to accurately recollect facts. While editing the military actions in the text, I did find some errors (if written history is to be accepted as truth), but for the most part Sprott was impressively accurate.

Based on his account of Stone's Battalion's (a portion of the 40th present at the battle) participation in the Battle of Chickamauga, my Father and I were able to follow the movement of that unit's brigade, under the command of Brigadier General Matthew D. Ector, over that battlefield. Sprott's few inaccuracies, as far as I can judge, were the result of lapses in memory. He mainly confused the names of battles in the latter half of the Atlanta Campaign, a confusing turn of events in its own right.

Another factor that sets this work apart, and probably the most compelling is that Sprott was clearly driven by his passion for his subject. This can be seen in all aspects of the text. He was driven by the memory of those who never had the chance to pen their memories to paper—those with whom Sprott shared his canteen, but were not so fortunate as to return home. Those men, he must have felt, were surely looking over his shoulder as he told their stories. He was committed to the legacy of the Army of Tennessee; and through his work, I believe the basic truth of the struggle in the West can be found. More importantly, the spirit of the common soldier and all his courage can finally be realized. My one hope for the publication of this piece is that it will aid in changing the incorrect and unfair stereotype of the "ignorant rebel."

It is important as one reads these pages to remember that the individuals mentioned were, for the most part, just boys. They were eighteen to twenty-four-year olds that should have been home on the farm courting young girls and contributing to their community. Sprott himself was twenty-two when he went off to war. Faced with the loss of their liberty, instead of farming or courting, they laid down the plow, left the girls behind, and marched to the battlefield. These were ordinary men that fought very extraordinary odds, and it is my hope that their legacy will endure.

Acknowledgements

There are a number of people I would like to thank for all their help on this project. In 1995 Mr. David Neel of Birmingham, Alabama gave me my first copy of Sprott's manuscript, as he had received it from Louis Smith, who was instrumental in bringing Sprott's work to public attention. I know of no more an intense student of the War Between the States than David. His frustration with not being more involved in the project provided inspiration for me to do my best so as to make him proud. I hope that I achieved that end. Dr. David Bowen, my editor/advisor in this project, is also deserving of thanks. Dr. Bowen "gracefully" edited my, oftentimes, three- to eight-page endnotes down to one or two lines. After getting over the initial shock of the editing process, I came to see Dr. Bowen's point. His input has been very beneficial. Also important to note is my boss, Mr. Michael Graham, and my co-workers in the university mail room for being so flexible. Most importantly, I would like to thank my parents. My mom was always there to listen to me when I hit a problem in my research. My dad actually flew from Connecticut in March of 1999 and took me to five battlefields in five days. I'm not sure if he has recovered from the bombardment of Civil War minutiae, but had it not been for him, I would have never been able to expand on my knowledge the way I did.

Though my grandfather, Robert Quist, has been gone for some years, I know he was looking over my shoulder as I worked on this project.

I would also like to thank all my pards in my reenactment unit, the 33rd Alabama Infantry Regiment Company E, for their interest and support. Their dedication and commitment to the preservation of this nation's history has been a wonderful source of inspiration.

Mr. Jim Blackwell, an Information Specialist of Eastern National Park and Monument Association, was a great help with my research on the Battle of Chickamauga. On a visit to the park, Mr. Blackwell showed me how to locate almost every position at which Stone's Battalion and Ector's Texas Brigade were engaged. Armed with Mr. Blackwell's information, I was much better equipped to understand one brigade's part in that great battle.

My uncle, Major K. Graham Fushak, provided me with several books that became very valuable reference material. he has been a great support in my writing.

Mr. Alan Pitts provided Appendix A for this work, through David Neel. Though I have only met Mr. Pitts once, I would like to thank him for his generosity in giving us this valuable information.

The Sumter County Historical Society funded this project; without the Society's help, Sprott's manuscript would still be relatively unknown.

There are many more that I should mention, but they know who they are and how much I appreciate their support.

Last, I would like to thank Judge Samuel Henry Sprott for leaving such a fine and enduring testimony of the War Between the States. I believe that it will stand as a beacon for all those who seek the truth about what happened in that terrible conflict.

Andrew Quist
Livingston, Alabama, 1999

CUSH:
A CIVIL WAR MEMOIR

SUMTER IN THE CIVIL WAR

Our Southern Home January 12, 1899

The heated political canvass of 1860 stirred the country as it had never before been stirred. While the doctrine of States Rights was almost universally held by the people of the South, at the same time there was a large and respectable element that was opposed to secession—some deeming it unwise and others opposing it from a strong devotion to the Union. And I will say right here that some of those who yelled loudest for secession and war, when the crisis came were like Job's war horse; they snuffed the battle from afar, while many of those who opposed it when the time came when their services were demanded did not hesitate or falter.

Another observation in this connection. My experience in the army, which doubtless will be corroborated by many others, was that generally the "bully" and "blowhard" at home was the coward in battle, while the quiet unobtrusive man, and who was thought to be a coward proved to be the bravest man in the command.

When secession became an accomplished fact there never was witnessed a more enthusiastic and unanimous support of a government. All past party differences were forgotten, and Dixie became one seething, boiling cauldron of patriotic enthusiasm.

And here I will remark that a similar condition of things existed in the North as in the South, viz: that a large and respectable number of people were opposed to war and coercion. To such an extent did this go that in the State of Illinois alone the Knights of the Golden Circle—an organization not opposed to the war but absolutely pledged to come to the aid of the South, numbered sixty thousand, among whom was claimed John A. Logan, afterwards a prominent general in the Federal army. Like causes produce like effects, and while the South became solidified for the cause of the Confederacy, the North in like manner became solidified for the Union, and thus it was that men who had sworn that an army marching to subdue the South would have to march over their dead bodies, were soon found marching with the invading army. So it was that each side was misled and deceived as to the true condition of things—the people of the North believing that there was a large and enthusiastic union party at the South, which only needed the presence of the Union army to assert itself, and the people of the South believing that there was a large and influential element at the North, not only opposed to the war, but who would actually enlist to fight with them for Southern independence. Both sides were sadly deceived as the sequel proved. Neither side thought the other in earnest about fighting.

Never was a country so poorly prepared for war as the South, and never did a people more nobly respond to all the demands made upon them. They entered into a war without arms or ammunition, there was not a place in the whole South where arms were manufactured. Without a navy and without credit. In addition to all this the geographical positions of the two sections were entirely dissimilar—the North with the dominion of Canada and British America behind it, stood like a man with his back to the wall, while the South was exposed front, rear and flanks, and was in the position of an ox surrounded by a pack of hungry wolves, some attacking in the front while others attacked in the rear and still others were tearing at the flanks.

But these things were not thought of by the masses in 1861. The fact is many of the early volunteers were afraid that the fun would all be over with before they got there. I heard of one fellow who offered his friend $50 to let him take his place in one of the first companies to go out just for sixty days, which he finally consented to do with the distinct understanding that he would give him back his place at the end of the sixty days. The poor fellow for four long years looked earnestly for his friend to come and claim his place, and he never came.

So it was the shock of war came and people were not prepared for it, but as I have stated they rallied heroically.

In April, I think it was, Capts. R. P. Blount and Jno. H. Dent left with their companies for Montgomery where the 5th Ala. under Col. R. E. Rodes was organized and from there they went to Pensacola and after spending some weeks there they were ordered to Virginia. Some time after these two companies left, Capt. A. S. VandeGraff carried a company from North Sumter to Virginia, and about the same time Capt. W. M. Stone with a company of cavalry left for the same place.

Men were anxious to volunteer and several other companies were organized during the summer of 1861, but when their services were tendered they were refused, the reason assigned being that there were no arms or accoutrements for them and they had to disband. So the summer and fall wore away and not until early in 1862 was there any demand for additional troops, and thus begins a new chapter.

Our Southern Home January 19, 1899

The fall of Forts Henry and Donelson and the consequent loss of Kentucky and Tennessee early in 1862 came as a great shock to the South. Gen. Albert Sidney Johnston fully realized the gravity of the situation and made every effort to meet the threatened danger.[1] During the fall of 1861 he called upon the Governors of Tennessee for 20,000, Mississippi 10,000, and Alabama 10,000, but Judah P. Benjamin, then Secretary of War, who had never set a squadron in the field and knew nothing about military affairs, countermanded the order, and indirectly reprimanded Gen. Johnston. So it was, that early in 1862 there was a call for more troops and over twenty new regiments were raised in a short while.

In February E. S. Gulley, a prominent planter, a man of intelligence and courage took steps to raise a company. On the 4th of March 1862, those who had volunteered in this company met at Intercourse and organized under the name of The South Sumter Guards; E. S. Gulley was elected Captain, Robert A. Brown 1st Lieutenant, James Cobbs 2nd Lieutenant and David C. Parker 3rd Lieutenant. Wm. R. McGowen was elected 1st Sergeant, Wm. H. James 2nd, S. H. Sprott 3rd, J. E. Daniel 4th, W. G. Cole 5th.

I can not recall the names of the corporals except S. D. Swain and Nathan Yarborough. The company was mustered in and sworn in the same day, but there being some informality about it, they were again sworn on the 17th day of March 1862, by H. S. Lide, mustering officer for the Confederate States. The following is a list of the members of the company, but also includes the names of those who joined subsequent to the organization. I will state that this list is made principally from memory, and I possibly have omitted some names.

Alexander, T. F.	Allen, John A.
Allison, W. S.	Anderson, John
Baines, S. R.	Banks, Jesse
Beavers, A. E.	Billups, John
Bolling, John	Bolling, Mark
Boon, J. C.	Boon, S. D.
Britt, J. A. J.	Brooks, Wm.
Bryan, B.	Bunyard, Isham
Bunyard, John	Burns, Patrick
Bustian, Wm.	Cole, W. G.
Daniel, Ed.	Daniel, Seth

Daugherty, N.
Dawkins, J. T.
Dearman, George
Dearman, Jas.
Dearman, N. B.
Donald, T. J.
Donald, T. T.
Donald, W. S.
Drummond, D.
Dunn, Jas
Everett, Henry
Ezell, E.
Ezell, George
Ezell, P.
Faulkner, J. D.
Ferrell, Robert
Fincher, H. S.
Flowers, G.
Fluker, Eugene
Franklin, H.
Graham, J. A.
Greene, Andrew
Greene, George
Greene, Isaiah
Grimes, J. D.
Hales, J. O.
Hammond, E. G.
Hammond, M. R.
Hammond, W. B.
Harper, E. F.
Harris, H. C.
Harrison, W. H.
Hitt, Clark
Hitt, James
Holder, Wm.
Howie, John
Irby, Wm.
James, W. H.
Jarman, Wm.
Jenkins, A. N.
Jones, J. A.
Kennon, Wm. F.
Kinsey, Jacob
Lancaster, Lewis
Lee, John
Lewis, W. C.
Lowery, M. H.
Maggard, Dave
Maggard, John
McDonald, John
McElroy, A. P.
McGowen, R. J.
McGowen, T. K.
McGowen, W. R.
McKenzie, Hector
Mobley, Alex
Nix, Sam'l
O'Neal, Hilliard
Owens, S. W.
Peteet, W. Y.
Peteet, Willis
Pratt, George
Praytor, John
Pulliam, J. L.

Quimby, Burrill	Quimby, Jonas
Roberts, John	Schimsky, Carl
Scott, John	Scott, Walter
Shaw, John	Shelby, John
Sloan, J. N.	Sprott, John
Sprott, S. H.	Stallings, James
Stallings, Wm.	Swann, S. D.
Tate, Wm.	Thetford, John
Thompson, Abe	Thompson, Frank
Vann, Ed	Vann, J. P.
Walker, E.	Walker, J. A.
Walker, Robt.	Watkins, O. F. H.
Watkins, Wm.	Webb, G. D.
Webb, Harvey	Webb, W. H.
Wheat, Bird	Whitfield, N. G.
Wideman, Robert	Wideman, Tom
Wilder, M. H.	Williams, Geo.
Williams, Robt.	Yarborough, N.

As already stated this list is made up almost entirely from memory and it may be that I have omitted some whose names ought to appear, or I may not have given the correct initials in every instance. I will state also that some of the names included in this list are of persons who did not originally go out with the company, some few of them being substitutes and others recruits who continued to come in during the war. In a subsequent article I will give the names of those who died or were killed, and when and where. If I have omitted any names from the list I would be glad to have my attention called to it.

Our Southern Home January 26, 1899

A few days after the organization, the company under Capt. Gulley went into camp at Gaston, occupying the old Female Academy. The organization of the company having been perfected, the same was reported to the Governor of Alabama and the following order received:

Executive Department
Mobile, Ala., March 10, 1862

Capt. E. S. Gulley: Your company, the "South Sumter Guards" is accepted this day. You will proceed at once to this city with your command and report on arrival to Brig. Gen'l Jones who will assign you to camp at Hall's Mill where you will be joined by other companies preparatory to the organization of a regiment. Transportation will be furnished by steamboat and railroad on your requisition.
Respectfully yours,
Jno. Gill Shorter.

A few days later the following order was received:

Office of Adjt. & Ins. Gen. Ala.
Montgomery, Ala., Mar. 1862

If the South Sumter Guards, Capt. Gulley, has not moved to Mobile, the order given by the Governor to do so is countermanded, and the company will, upon the order of Col. A. A. Coleman, rendezvous at or near Demopolis.

By order of the Governor.
G. W. Goldwaite
Adjt. & Ins. Gen. Ala.

It having been ascertained as before stated, that there being some informality in mustering the company into the service of the Confederate States, the men were again sworn in on the 17th of March. The company remained at Gaston about a week, when we received orders from Col. Coleman to proceed to Demopolis by steamboat from Black's Bluff.

Old soldiers will recall with a smile their first experience in army life. Every man had one or two blankets, one or two and sometimes three quilts—and two suits of clothes with underwear in proportion, all of which would fill a medium sized trunk. As friends and neighbors brought wagons to transport men and baggage to the river there was but little trouble with the baggage.

This company was made up of country boys who had been brought up on the farm, many of whom had never been further from home than Livingston, and had never been on a steamboat before. It was amusing to hear the quaint remarks some of them would make about different things that struck them as being new or novel. About the 25th of March we arrived at Demopolis and camped at the Fair Grounds. Capt. Gulley's company being first organized and received into the service of the Confederate States was known as Co. A in the 40th Ala. Regiment of Infantry.

On the 4th of April, 1862, we were joined by a company from Pickens County, under command of Capt. E. D. Willett, which became Co. B. of the 40th Ala. While at Demopolis we lost our first man, Ed. Vann from near Cuba. He was taken with pneumonia and lived but a few days. He was an excellent man and doubtless would have made a fine soldier had he lived. His death cast a gloom over the camp. A few days after the arrival of Capt. Willett's company from Pickens, Capt. W. A. C. Jones with his company from Sumter arrived. This company became Co. C. Soon afterwards two companies from Choctaw County arrived; one under Capt. A. G. Campbell, which became Co. D and the other under Capt. Ed. Marsh which

8

became Co. E.

In a few days the Fair Grounds presented a lively scene, drilling being the order of the day. On all sides you could see squads moving and hear the words "hep, hep, hep," "one, two, one, two," "right wheel," "left wheel," "halt," etc.

While at Gaston, Mr. M. A. Marshall, who owned a blacksmith shop at that place had a large steel circular saw cut up and made into knives and gave each man one. Some very exaggerated statements had been made about the havoc wrought by Wheat's Louisiana Tigers at Manassas with bowie knives, and it was thought that we could do the same with Marshall's knives. It was not long, however, before they were discarded, as we soon learned that with modern fire-arms it rarely happens that opposing sides get near enough to even use the bayonet.

It may be interesting to some of the old soldiers to give the names of the different officers in the companies assembled at Demopolis, which I do from memory:

Co. A —E. S. Gulley, Captain; R. A. Brown, 1st Lieut.; Jas. Cobbs, 2nd Lieutenant; D. C. Parker, 3rd Lieut.

Co. B —E. D. Willett, Captain; John T. Terry, 1st Lieut.; James A. Latham, 2nd Lieut.; James H. Weir, 3rd Lieut.

Co. C —W. A. C. Jones, Captain; A. J. Phares, 1st Lieut.; T. M. Brunson, 2nd Lieutenant; J. W. Monette, 3rd Lieutenant.

Co. D —A. G. Campbell, Captain; Frank Blakeney, 1st Lieut.; V. R. Williams, 2nd Lieut.; name of the 3rd Lieutenant forgotten.

Co. E —Ed Marsh, Captain; Jos. Woodward 1st Lieut.; Ed. Ward, 2nd Lieut.; W. E. Yancey, 3rd Lieut.

Soon after these companies arrived at Demopolis Clarence H. Ellerbee, senior captain of the corps of cadets at the University of Alabama, was assigned to duty with us as drill officer, and became Adjutant of the regiment. He was a model officer and Adjutant—a brave and gallant soldier. He passed through the war unscathed until

9

the last battle at Bentonville, N.C., where he was killed.

On the 17th of April companies A and B received orders to proceed to Mobile. We marched down to the river. When the steamer *Cherokee* arrived we found the Fowler's Battery from Tuskaloosa, with about 150 men was aboard, and only one company could be taken. So Co. A went aboard and Co. B returned to camp.

Our Southern Home February 2, 1899

About April 18, 1862, we arrived at Mobile and were quartered in an old cotton warehouse, where we remained about eight days. The old house was infested with rats of all sizes and ages, and they seemed to take delight in running across the faces of the boys after lights were out. The companies left at Demopolis having arrived, the whole command moved, on the 26th day of April, to Dog River, some four or five miles from the city and occupied houses that had been used by the operatives in a factory that had been located there. The camp was known as Cantonment Walter. The houses we occupied were four room cottages two below and two above about sixteen feet square. Each room was occupied by ten or twelve men. Soon after we arrived at Cantonment Walter, measles broke out, and as the rooms were crowded—sometimes ten men were lying on the floor at one time—it was attended with great fatality. Capt. Jones lost out of his company seventeen men in a few weeks. It is a sad but notorious fact that more men died from measles and diseases incident to camp life than were killed in battle.

The regiment was soon after completed by the addition of the following companies:

Co. F —From Choctaw and Mobile, T. W. Coleman, Capt.; T. K. Irwin, 1st Lieut.; J. H. Knighton, 2nd Lieut.; Kelly, 3rd Lieut.

Co. G —From Pickens, Hugh Summerville, Capt.; T. O. Stone, 1st Lieut.; Loftin, 2nd Lieut.; Hamiter, 3rd Lieut.

Co. H —From Perry, C. C. Crowe, Capt.; C. H. B. Hicks, 1st

Lieut.; J. C. Moore, 2nd Lieut.; name of 3rd Lieut. not remembered.

Co. I —From Covington, Hiram Gantt, Capt.; Blackford, 1st Lieut.; Schafer, 2nd Lieut.; name of 3rd Lieut. not remembered.

Co. K —From Sumter, A. M. Moore, Captain; Abram Larkin, 1st Lieut.; W. B. Bingham, 2nd Lieut.; Joe Patton, 3rd Lieut.

It might be interesting to note here the changes that took place in the company officers of the three companies from Sumter during the war up to the period of the reorganization of the Army of Tennessee in 1865, when the 19th Ala. and the 40th Ala. were consolidated. In Co. A, R. A. Brown resigned on account of ill health, and James Cobbs became 1st Lieut. D. C. Parker became 2nd Lieut. and W. R. McGowen was elected 3rd Lieutenant. Subsequent to this, Capt. E. S. Gulley was promoted to Major, and James Cobbs became Captain. There being a vacancy in the lieutenancy, S. H. Sprott was elected, and Lieutenant McGowen resigning on account of ill health, and Lieut. Parker being on detached service, S. H. Sprott became 1st Lieutenant, D. C. Parker remained 2nd Lieutenant, and W. Y. Peteet was elected 3rd Lieutenant. Lieut. Parker resigned and W. P. Hall was elected 3rd Lieut., Peteet becoming 2nd Lieut.

In Co. C, 1st Lieut. A. J. Phares resigned and T. M. Brunson became 1st Lieut., J. W. Monette became 2nd Lieut., and James Hartsfield was elected 3rd Lieut. Capt. W. A. C. Jones being transferred to the Engineer Department, T. M. Brunson became Capt., J. W. Monette 1st Lieut., James Hartfield 2nd Lieut., and N. E. Thomas was elected 3rd Lieutenant.

In Co. K, 1st Lieut. Abram Larkin resigned on account of ill health and W. B. Bingham became 1st Lieut., Joe Patton 2nd Lieut., and B. B. Sanders was elected 3rd Lieut. Lieut. Patton died during the siege of Vicksburg, and B. B. Sanders became 2nd Lieut., and T. R. M. Simmons was elected 3rd Lieut. A great many changes took place in the other Companies of the regiment, but as these reminiscences are intended only to relate the part taken by soldiers from

Sumter in the war, the others will only be mentioned incidentally in connection with these three companies.

The regiment, having the requisite number of companies, was about the 1st of May, 1862, organized by the election of A. A. Coleman, of Sumter, as Colonel; John H. Highley of Mobile, Lieut. Col.; Devereaux Hopkins, of Choctaw, Major, but he declining to accept the position another election was subsequently held, and Capt. T. O. Stone of Pickens was elected Major. C. H. Ellerbee of Dallas was appointed Adjutant; and B. C. Whitfield, of Marengo, Sergeant Major; Dr. Geo. J. Colgin, of Sumter, was appointed Surgeon; and Dr. John Merriweather, of Green, Assistant Surgeon; T. H. Lake, of Sumter, was appointed Regimental Quarter Master and was afterwards succeeded by R. H. Baker, of Selma. W. H. Baker, of Mobile, was appointed Regimental Commissary, and Wesley Dodson, Assistant Commissary.

Rev. Joseph Baker, a Methodist minister, was appointed Chaplain but resigned some months afterwards and was succeeded by Rev. A. D. McVoy. The regiment being thus completed and organized.

The 36th, 38th, and 40th Ala. regiments were put in the same brigade under Brigadier Gen'l Jones who was subsequently succeeded by Brigadier Gen'l Cummings. Sometimes after this the 18th Ala. was added to the brigade.

These regiments together with the 3rd and 4th Florida and 27th Miss. together with several batteries constituted the army in and around Mobile, and the entire force was under the command of Maj. Gen'l John H. Forney. On the 21st of July the 40th Ala. moved from Cantonment Walker to Camp Marshall Austill, which was about a mile and a half south of Mobile.

On October 8th, the regiment moved from Camp Marshall Austill to Camp Forney, some two or three miles from Mobile, on the Spring Hill Road where it remained until Dec. 2nd, 1862. When the regiment was first organized the men were armed with old smooth bore muskets which had been changed from flint and steel to percussion guns. They were old and rusty and it took a vast amount of rubbing to get them bright.

Our Southern Home February 9, 1899

Early in the fall we were armed with Enfield rifles just received from England. The regiment was well drilled and disciplined and during the fall of that year numbered about one thousand men.

In giving a list of the members of Co. A. of the 40th Ala., in a previous issue I omitted Monroe Hearn and David Watson. I think this completes the list though it is possible that I may have still omitted some names.

On looking over the roll I find that this company had first and last 127 men including officers, and out of that number the following were killed or died.

T. F. Alexander died at Mobile, Ala., in 1862; Wm. S. Allison killed at the battle of New Hope Church, May 24th, 1864; John Anderson killed at the battle of Noonday Creek, June 15th, 1864; John Billups killed at the battle of Bentonville, Feb. 19, 1865; John Bolling killed at the battle of Bentonville, Feb. 19, 1865; J. A. J. Britt died at Camp Forney near Mobile, Alabama in the fall of 1862; S. D. Boon died in prison; John Bunyard killed at the battle of Chickamauga, Sept. 19th, 1863; Wm. Brooks killed at the battle of Bentonville, Feb. 19th, 1865; John Dawkins killed at the battle of Chickamauga, Sept. 19th, 1863; N. B. Dearman killed at the battle of New Hope Church, May 24th, 1864; D. Drummond died at Mobile in 1862; W. S. Donald died at Mobile in 1862; T. J. Donald died at home in 1862; James Dunn died at Atlanta, Ga. in 1864; Henry Everett died at Mobile in 1862; H. S. Fincher killed at Atlanta, July 28th, 1864; Eugene Fluker died at home; J. D. Grimes died at Rolling Fork, Miss., in1862; W. H. Harrison died at same place about the same time; E. G. Hammond killed at Chickamauga, Sept. 19th, 1863; J. O. Hales died place not remembered; H. C. Harris killed at the battle of Resaca, May 14th, 1864; Monroe Hearn died at Jackson, Miss. in 1862; Wm. Irby killed at the battle of Missionary Ridge, Nov. 25th, 1863; J. A. Jones died at home in 1864; W. C. Lewis died in prison at Rock Island, Ill.; John Lee died, place not known; T. K. McGowen died at Dalton, Ga. in 1864; Samuel Nix killed at Vicksburg during the siege; Willis Peteet killed at the battle of Bentonville, Feb. 19th, 1865; John Praytor killed at the battle of Bentonville, Feb. 19th, 1865; Jonas Quimby died, place not remembered; John Shaw died at home; John Scott died at Mobile, Ala. in 1862; J. N. Sloan died at Vicksburg during the siege; John Shelby killed at the battle of Missionary Ridge, Nov. 25th, 1863; Wm.Tate died, place not remembered; Ed Vann died at Demopolis, Ala., a few weeks after the company was organized; J. P. Vann was accidentally killed at Mobile by John Praytor in 1864; Wm. Bustain was accidentally killed a few weeks before Vann was killed, by being knocked from the top of a box car, between Montgomery and Mobile; Wm. Watkins killed at Atlanta, July 28th, 1864; O. F. H. Watkins was mortally wounded, and died some weeks afterwards at Meridian, Miss., 1863. He had been in the hospital there and being convalescent was put on guard to protect some government property, and while in the discharge of his duty was shot by some of the paroled soldiers of the Vicksburg Army. W. H. Wilder died, place not remembered. Thomas Wideman was wounded at Chickamauga, Sept. 19th, 1863, recovered sufficiently to come home, but died soon afterwards. In addition to this, quite a number were wounded, some maimed for life, while others were slightly wounded and soon returned to duty.

OFF TO MISSISSIPPI-PROVOST DUTY

[continued from <u>Our Southern Home</u> February 9, 1899]

On Dec. 2nd, 1862, Col. Coleman received orders to have his regiment ready to move in two hours for Grenada, Miss. The battle of Corinth had been fought and lost and our army was falling back in the direction of Grenada and we were to be dispatched as rapidly as possible to reinforce them.[2] When the order came the men were wild with excitement as they had long desired active service rather than garrison duty. Tents were taken down, surplus baggage was thrown away and even then we had twice as much as we ought to have had, and in less than two hours, we were on our way to Mobile, marching in splendid style, preceded by our excellent brass band. We arrived at the depot and found awaiting us a train of box-cars and soon left for Meridian where we arrived at 3 a.m. and disembarked in a cold rain sleepy and hungry as it was next to impossible to sleep in the crowded box-cars and we had not had anything to eat since the morning before. We stopped not far from the depot, built fires and tried to make ourselves as comfortable as we could, under the circumstances. After daylight we had issued to us some pickled pork and crackers, hard enough and old enough looking to have been with Noah on his cruise in the Ark. We soon learned to make "cush," which was done by putting crackers in a frying pan with water and a little gravy, and keeping it over the fire until the crackers were perfectly soft, which made a dish not to be despised by a hungry man. But all efforts to find some substitute for coffee were fruitless. The villainous compound known as corn meal coffee, which was made by parching the meal brown and then putting it in a camp kettle and boiling as we do coffee, was enough to turn the stomach of any one but a hungry soldier. "Ugh!" I can taste it yet.

During the afternoon of the 3rd we were placed aboard another train of box cars; the one assigned to our company had been used for the transportation of horses and had not been cleaned out; it was covered with filth three or four inches deep. Fortunately there was a large pile of oat straw nearby and the gentleman to whom it belonged gave us permission to take as much of it as we wanted; and we took it all. It was fortunate for us that we got the straw as we were in the car all that night, all day the next day and until midnight, when we arrived at Canton, Miss., as the enemy had fallen back. On the trip from Meridian to Canton and then back to Jackson we were cooped up in these box cars for nearly forty-eight hours, without an opportunity to cook any, so we ate fat pickled pork raw with our "hard tack" as it was called, and I never tasted a sweeter morsel in my life. So much for that most excellent "sauce" hunger, and a digestive apparatus like an ostrich. After reaching Jackson we were allowed to get off and cook breakfast which we did by sticking a piece of meat on a stick and broiling it before the fire letting the grease drop into a tin plate, to which was added a little water and then the crackers added, and we had our "cush." This was all the cooking we could do as our cooking utensils had been left behind and had not yet been received. After we had finished breakfast we were ordered down the New Orleans R. R. about two miles near a creek where we found Vaughn's Tennessee Brigade, consisting of the 79th, 80th and 81st Tenn. encamped. Here we remained for about ten days drilling and doing guard and provost duty in Jackson.

16

While near Jackson we did provost and guard duty in the city. A company would go on duty at 6 o'clock p.m. and remain until 6 p.m. the next day. The company would be divided into three reliefs and these would be on duty two hours each. Our company under Capt. Gulley marched in one afternoon and relieved the company that had been on duty for the previous twenty-four hours. I was put in charge of a squad of five men, going on duty about 12 o'clock at night with orders to patrol the lower part of the city where the railroad yards were located. Our orders were to halt every man we met and make him give an account of himself and if he could not do this, he was to be arrested and taken to head-quarters where he would be confined in the guard house. How completely all civil rights are overridden and stamped out by the iron hand of war.

While in the performance of our duty I heard three or four shots fired in rapid succession followed by screams and cries of some one as if in terrible distress. As our orders required us to patrol the place and keep order I immediately double-quicked my squad in the direction from which the cries for help came. We soon reached the bank of the Pearl River near the railroad bridge. The Mississippi state troops were camped near by, and an old Captain with long grey beard was standing in front of his tent, and upon inquiring what and where the trouble was, he told me that it was across the river. We started to cross the railroad bridge but some of the men becoming giddy we retraced our steps and passed up the bank of the river to the public bridge, some distance above. After crossing, the cries for help continuing, I halted my men and ordered them to load their guns and then forming as for a skirmish we proceeded in the direction from which the cries came and in a few minutes saw a light on a small elevation in the swamp. On approaching within a few yards of the place we saw a large tent with a fire in front and between this and the tent a man walking back and forth calling as loud as he could, "come here," "somebody come here." Halting my men I stepped up and asked him what the trouble was; he told me that two women had been shot; that he and one of the women were sitting on a trunk or box in front of the fire and a friend and the other woman were sitting on the opposite side when some person or persons had slipped up under cover of the darkness and fired, both women being struck and the tent riddled. Lying on a mattress in front of the tent near the fire I found a young girl apparently not more than eighteen years of age. She was a beautiful blue-eyed blonde with regular, almost child-like features, and her dress indicated that she was or had been more than an ordinary "street walker." I observed a little blood on her night gown, and upon opening it I discovered a little purple spot near the left breast, where the bullet had penetrated. I was but a boy, but had seen enough of death to know from the pallor on her face and the region of her wound that she was beyond all earthly aid. I then turned my attention to the other woman, who was lying just inside of the tent on a mattress. She was older, coarser and evidently more hardened than the other. I found that she had a ghastly wound in her head and I soon saw that I could do nothing for her. When I turned around to look at the young girl she had ceased breathing and looking at her beautiful placid face you would have thought that she had only fallen asleep. The other woman lived until the next morning. I sent two men back to report to Capt. Gulley and ask him for instructions. Soon after these men left, a crowd of tough characters came, some of them drunk and all of them more or less disposed to quarrel, and it was with the greatest difficulty that I could preserve order. Finally just about day light the messengers sent to Capt. Gulley returned and informed me that our jurisdiction only extended to the Pearl River, and to report to head-quarters. This affair was shrouded in mystery. I don't know that any investigation was ever had, or any notice ever taken of it except a short notice in the paper the next morning stating that two women had been shot and killed last night across the river in the swamp. I regret that I cannot recall the names of all the men who were with me that night, but after a lapse of more than thirty-six years I find it impossible to recall but two: M. R. Hammond was one, and John Shelby was another.

On Dec. 16th, 1862 orders were received for our regiment to proceed at once to Columbus, Miss., to repel a raid of federal troops coming from the direction of Corinth. On the next day we marched to Jackson and as usual got into box cars and started for Meridian where we arrived early on the morning of the 18th. The weather was very cold and the men suffered from both cold and hunger. We left Meridian the same day and arrived at Columbus on the morning of the 19th and got off near the railroad bridge over the Bigbee River at that place. On the trip from Meridian to Columbus which was at night, an incident occurred which is worth relating. It seems that the commanding officers had been informed or had reason to suspect the loyalty of the engineer in charge of the engine pulling the train; they apprehended that he would either ditch the train or run past Artesia and run us into the Yankee fences some distance up the M. & O. R. R., who would have us at a fearful disadvantage. So Capt. T. W. Coleman, who was noted for his nerve and courage, was placed in the cab with the engineer with instructions to shoot him down if any thing went wrong. But as I have stated we arrived at Columbus safely on the morning of the 19th. Late that evening we marched through the city in splendid style with brass band playing and flag flying, and proceeded to the Fair Grounds, where we went into camp.

Not long after getting into camp, Bogan C. Harvell [sic] came to see us, and as nearly everyone in the regiment from Choctaw and Sumter knew him, and knowing how fond he was of speaking he was called on to make a speech, which he finally consented to do, but I must reserve this for the next issue as it would make this too long.

Bogan C. Harrell (not Harvell) as the types made me say last week was one of unique characters of South Sumter. During the fifties he was a standing candidate for the Legislature to represent Sumter County, was voted for at each election for Governor, for Congress, for State Senator, and almost every other office within the gift of the people. Bogan said that he got votes enough but they were so badly scattered that they didn't do him any good; he thought if he could have concentrated his votes that he would have been elected. He closed his speech at Gaston during one of his campaigns as follows: "I was born in poverty, brought up on the pot-hooks of posterity, I took an everlasting whack at eternity and jumped off with a whoopee," jumping as far as he could into the crowd as he closed. Bogan C. Harrell was a kind hearted, genial, pleasant man. He was always in demand at the Camp meetings that were held annually near the Choctaw line not far from the Speed place, to lead in the singing in which he took great delight. He had a song of his own composition, which he would sing with great fervor. I remember when quite a small boy hearing him sing this song one night at Camp meeting. It was a beautiful night, and quite a crowd collected near his cabin, tent it was called, to hear him sing. He sang all the hymns he knew and wound up with his own production. All I remember was as follows:

"The devil is mad,
And Bogan is glad.
And I want to go to glory,
Oh, hallelujah!"

And there were about sixteen more verses like unto this. It can well be imagined how eager the boys from Choctaw and Sumter who either knew him or knew of him from character, were to hear him speak. There were a lot of empty cracker boxes lying around and these were soon piled up, and after the band played a piece Bogan mounted the improvised rostrum and launched forth. I can only recall the opening remarks as follows:

"Fellow soldiers of Alabamy. When I seen you marching through the City of Columbus today with yur flag flying and yur brass band playing I was proud that I was from Alabamy but am ashamed to say that I belong to the Mississippi flop-eared melish... Boys" he said, placing his hands about the waistband of his breeches— "from thar up old Bogan is as brave as they ever make 'em, but them thar critters—pointing down to his legs, durn 'em I cant keep 'em from running to save my life." He concluded his speech by saying if he was a little younger he would get transferred to our regiment but as his time was nearly out, the state troops being called out only for ninety days, he thought he could do the Confederacy more good by going home and raising corn and potatoes, and looking after the women and children, than he could by fighting. There were a good many all over the South that felt a good deal like Bogan did, and they didn't have age on their side as he had either.

Many of them who hurrahed for secession were like Buck Anderson when some of his friends were urging him to volunteer and he was not inclined to do so and when reminded that he voted for secession said, "Yes but I voted for peaceable secession; you fellows told me that them Yankees wouldn't fight and we wouldn't have any war."

VICKSBURG

[continued from Our Southern Home February 23, 1899]

On Dec. 26, 1862, we received an order from Gen. Pemberton to report at Vicksburg at once. Gen. Sherman, with a large force had effected a landing on the Yazoo River near Chickasaw Bayou. If he could force our lines at that place he could very easily get in the rear of Vicksburg. The obstructions at Snyder's Bluff could be removed and a good base of operations secured. It was highly important, therefore, that reinforcements should be hurried forward as rapidly as possible to prevent the success of this movement on the part of the Federal forces. The regiment broke camp the night of the 26th and marched to the railroad and took the train at 4 o'clock A. M. on the morning of the 27th, in a perfect down pour of rain. We arrived at Meridian about 4 P. M. the next day. For some unexplained cause we were detained here until the next day at 11 A. M., when we took the train for Vicksburg, arriving at that place Dec. 30th at 8 P. M., taking nearly four days to make a trip that ought to have been made in one.

During this entire time the men were cooped up in box cars, the weather cold and disagreeable, and no opportunity to cook what little "grub" we had, hence we ate our bacon raw, and masticated our hard tack as best we could. Under all these trying circumstances the men were cheerful, full of fun and frolic and eager to get to the front. In about two hours after our arrival at Vicksburg we were ordered to march to Chickasaw Bayou where a battle had been fought that day and a glorious victory won by the Confederates under Gen. Stephen

D. Lee.[3] We marched up the river road along the base of Walnut Hills in perfect silence, as at many points we were within shelling distance of the enemy's guns. It was very dark and it took a long time to reach the line of battle, which we did about 3 o'clock A. M., when we were posted in support of a battery. A renewal of the fight was expected next morning, but instead of a battle a flag of truce was sent in by Gen. Sherman asking permission to bury his dead who were strewn all over the field in our front. After they had buried their dead—about two hundred in number—the truce having expired, skirmishing was resumed and a spattering fire was kept up along the entire picket line. Later in the day a force from our lines under Gen. Dabney H. Maury advanced and drove the enemies across the bayou in the direction of the Lake plantation, where under the protection of their gun-boats they embarked and returned to Miliken's Bend on the Mississippi River. We spent the day in the trenches, and bivouacked in a narrow valley just back of our line of battle. The rain came down in torrents and we were without shelter save our blankets; the soil was soft and black, and the best we could do was to sit around on stumps and brush, with our blankets around us. We had slept but little the night before, had been in line of battle all day and now sleep was impossible.

The next day was clear and cold, and after it was ascertained that the enemy had disappeared from our front, we were moved back to a high hill in our rear in an open field, where the wind had full sweep. Everyone who soldiered around Vicksburg will remember the character of the soil—mud—mud—everywhere.

After we got possession of the Lake place where the enemy landed, our men discovered several barrels of pickled pork in the river where the enemy had rolled it, not having time to get it on board their boats. Our boys soon fished it out and we had full rations for a few days.

I will state in this connection that while we were camped near

Vicksburg we had the poorest rations we had during the war and this too in a section of country filled with the finest, fattest cattle and untold quantities of corn. Each man received a pound of the poorest, bluest beef that was ever seen; three-quarters of a pound of meal with the bran in it; and a gill of sour molasses caused by being under water for a considerable length of time and this was to last him twenty four hours. The beef cattle were kept in a pen near Vicksburg without anything to eat and the rule was to kill those that could not get up; those that were strong enough to get up were spared for another day.

We had no way of sifting the bran out of our meal, even if we could have spared it, and so it was cooked with the bran in it, and without salt and we used what little we got to season our beef. It is calculated to make an old soldier smile to read of the sufferings of our soldiers for a few days in Cuba. I will also add that while encamped near Vicksburg we received our first installments of "Greybacks." We had heard of "Greenbacks and Greybacks," but had not seen either up to this time. If the younger generation wish to know more about this matter, let them inquire of some old soldier as to the difference between the two articles.

Our Southern Home March 2, 1899

I will suspend the narrative of the movements of the 40th Alabama to give a list of the names of the members of Co. "C," commanded when it first went out by Capt. W. A. C. Jones, which list has been furnished by Mr. W. A. Altman, who, with the assistance of two or three comrades has been enabled to furnish almost a complete list. But as stated before these lists are made out from memory, and it is quite likely that some names may have been omitted. I will state that my attention has been called by friend, W. R. McGowen, to the fact that I omitted several names from Co. "A," as follows:

Tom Greene wounded at the battle of Bentonville, N.C. on March

19th, 1865, left on the field of battle and never heard of afterwards; Jas. L. Hale who died at Vicksburg, Miss., a few days after the surrender of that place; and J. A. Patterson who died at Mobile, Ala. in 1862.

I have in a previous issue given a list of the commissioned officers of Co. "C," and it is not necessary to repeat it. The following is a list of the non-commissioned officers and privates.

Altman, W. A.	Anderson, Buck
Armstrong, Hunter	Armstrong, W. C.
Augle, Joshua	Barker, B. S.
Barker, Hamp	Batton, William
Bell, James	Benson, *
Bevill, Bolivar	Blakeney, Jack
Blount, W. H.	Bobbitt, *
Buckalew, Ira	Carroll, Joshua
Copeland, N.	Culpepper, A.
Culpepper, Ben	Culpepper, H.
Culpepper, Hubert	Culpepper, James
Culpepper, M.	Culpepper, Mack
Culpepper, O.	Culpepper, Pet
Culpepper, Phillip	Cunningham, T. R.
Cusack, J. E.	Davidson, Joe
Davidson, W. R.	Dean, Aleck
Dill, Sam	Dodson, Wes
Eads, Robert	Elder, Robert
Evans, Sam	Faulkner, J.
Flowers, J. B.	
Ford, William	Freeman, J.
Freeman, John	Freeman, S.
Garrison, George	Gatewood, Ellis
Gatewood, Jas.	Glover, Wesley
Glover, Zeke	Gooden, George

Gooden, Jas.

Hardin, Joe

Harris, H. C.

Hartsfield, George

Henderson, W.

Hoard, Oscar

James, John

Jowers, Dock

Lacy, Steve

Lockard, P. S.

Maiden, Ed.

Matthews, J. B.

Mayes, Joe

Murphy, M.

Parker, Jack

Peaton, A. G.

Rainer, Berry

Rainer, F.

Rainer, Jas.

Rushing, A.

Sanders, Elias

Sanders, Jasper

Sims, Frank

Solly, Eb.

Speed, Joe

Thomas, N. E.

Thrash, Jack

Tureman, Perry

Watson, F.

Watts, W. H.

Williams, H. S.

Wilson, Alex.

Yarborough, James

Hardin, Hugh

Hardin, Mad.

Harris, Meck.

Hartsfield, Jas.

Hendricks, Tom

Horton, John

Johnson, Tom

Kennedy, William

Lewis, A. G.

Mahan, J.

Maiden, William

Mayes, Dr. J. M.

McAlpine, W.

O'Connor, D.

Parker, John

Peaton, W. F.

Rainer, Charles

Rainer, George

Rix, Major

Rushing, C.

Sanders, J.

Sheram, Nat

Sims, James

Speed, Ben

Springstead, *

Thrash, Eli

Torry, Geo. W.

Warner, Wm.

Watson, Lee

Welsh, D.

Willis, *

Yarborough, D.

Yarborough, John

Including commissioned officers, this Company had on its rolls, first and last, one hundred and twenty-one men. I can only give a partial list of the died and killed.

John Yarborough, the first man belonging to the 40th Ala. killed on the battle field, belonged to Co. "C." He was killed March 25, 1863, in a skirmish with the enemy on Little Deer Creek, Miss. Steve Lacey was killed at Vicksburg during the siege. Jim Rainer was killed at the battle of Resaca, Ga., May 14th, 1864. He was but a boy but was fighting like a hero when he fell. I was near him, and as we fell back his father and brother attempted to bring him off, but being unable to do so—there being no litter near at hand, they laid him gently down, and his father, George Rainer, with tears streaming down his face, turned sadly away and left his dead boy lying near where he had fallen. He in turn gave up his life on the battle field of Bentonville, N.C., March 19, 1865. At the same time and place (Bentonville, March 19, 1865) Jack Thrash, another good soldier of this company, was killed. Both Rainer and Thrash were middle-aged men and made splendid soldiers. Jack Sanders died at Mobile in 1862. Jasper Sanders and Elias Sanders died, but the time and place is not remembered. John James died at Mobile in 1862. Henry C. Harris, who went out with this company, was transferred to Co. A. and as heretofore stated was killed at the battle of Resaca, May 14th, 1864. John Freeman was killed at the battle of Peach Tree Creek, Ga., July 28, 1864. Robert Eads died at Vicksburg during the siege. Alexander Dean died at Dalton, Ga., early in 1864. This is but a partial list of the died and killed of this company—perhaps not a third.

If the relatives and friends of those who died or were killed would furnish me with the data as to time and place of death, and whether killed or died from disease, I will take pleasure in recording the same that future generations may know the great sacrifices our people made in their struggle for independence. These brave men who laid down their lives on the battle field or in the hospital deserve to have their names perpetuated and handed down to posterity as a rich legacy, and those of us who survive ought to see that this is done.

I hope that different members of Co. "K" will make an effort to get up a list of that company.

Our Southern Home March 9, 1899

The 40th Alabama remained on the hill in rear of the battle field of Chickasaw Bayou about forty-eight hours, without tents or shelter or any kind, and nothing to burn except green wood, mostly black locust and walnut. About January 5th we moved down into the valley near the bayou and went into camp in an open field. We got our tents and cooking utensils and were quite comfortable considering the rations we received and the wood we had to burn.

We remained at this camp, called Camp Timmons in honor of Col. Timmons of the 2nd Texas who was killed while gallantly leading his regiment in the battle of Chickasaw Bayou, until Feb. 17th. On this day, just about dark, and while the rain was pouring down in torrents, we were ordered to move up the road two or three miles to a bridge across Chickasaw Creek. It had rained a great deal and the road was almost impassable owing to the character of the soil and the immense amount of hauling over it, that being the main road between Snyder's Bluff on the Yazoo River, where the corn from that river and Sunflower River, was unloaded from boats, in Vicksburg. The mud was knee deep, and it was so dark that you could not see a man a few feet from you. Many of the men lost their shoes and some their hats, while all were covered with mud. There were many mysterious things done during the war, but this move was the most unaccountable and inexcusable of which I ever knew. We were marching out at night in the rain through the mud leaving our tents standing, to take the place of another regiment that in like manner had been moved further up the line, with no enemy in our front, or nearer than Miliken's Bend, some ten or twelve miles away, across the Mississippi River.

Some General sitting in his comfortable quarters in Vicksburg had doubtlessly directed his Adjutant General to issue the order that day without thinking or caring about the condition of the road, or the comfort of the men. But such is soldier life; orders must be obeyed it matters not how useless or foolish it may be. We did not arrive at the bridge until about 11 o'clock at night, and as soon as we arrived there Co. A. under Lieut. W. R. McGowen was ordered on picket duty on the levee of Yazoo River, some half a mile or more from the bridge. We remained at this camp until March the 19th and just before leaving we witnessed the first military execution we had ever seen. At the battle of Chickasaw Bayou a young man by the name of Brown was captured by a Louisiana regiment to which he had belonged, and from which he had deserted at Fort Jackson below New Orleans. He gave the enemy valuable information as to the number of men, guns, etc., in the forts. After the fall of the forts and the capture of the city of New Orleans the troops that had been captured were exchanged and were in the Confederate army at Vicksburg. When Brown was captured he was immediately recognized by his former comrades though he was in Federal uniform. He was tried by a court martial and sentenced to be shot. The execution took place in a little cove surrounded by hills on three sides, and in the presence of the entire division of five or six thousand men. It was a beautiful day about the middle of March. The sun was shining, the birds singing, and a tinge of green among the trees all indicated the approach of spring. In the center of the little cove or valley a grave had been dug. The soldiers had formed around on three sides of a square, and in a few minutes a wagon was driven up in which was the prisoner sitting on his coffin, and beside him a Catholic priest. The wagon surrounded by the provost guard, was stopped near where our command stood. The prisoner and the priest got out and the coffin was taken out and placed just in front of the grave. I was struck with the youthful appearance of the prisoner; he did not appear to be more than eighteen or twenty years of age. His beardless face was pale, but aside from this he was calm and self-possessed. He was dressed in a new Federal uniform, with a dark over-shirt—his coat unbuttoned, exposing his breast fully. He was seated on his coffin with his back to the grave, his hands tied behind him. After the priest had concluded his services, he retired, and the captain of the provost guard stepped forward with a handkerchief to blindfold him, but the young fellow shook his head indicating that he did not want to be blind-folded, whereupon the captain stepped back to his place with the guard who were to fire the fatal volley.

The prisoner took a long look around, as if anxious to take in as much of this world as he could before leaving it. The captain gave the command "ready," whereupon the guns were raised and brought to the shoulder. The prisoner straightened himself up, threw back his shoulders, leaning himself forward and said in a distinct voice, looking straight into the muzzles of the guns, "Good day, gentlemen, take good aim." Then in rapid succession came the commands—"Aim," "Fire." There was a crash. The blood spurted from his breast and he sank to the ground, thus paying the penalty of his great crime.

The recital of such a scene is not pleasant, but in recording the incidents that go to make up history and depicting the soldier's life in time of war, it is frequently necessary to record events of a harrowing character.

Our Southern Home March 23, 1899

We remained in camp near Chickasaw Creek until March 19th, 1863, when we were ordered to Hayne's Bluff on the Yazoo River just above Snyder's Bluff. Both points were well fortified, and in addition strong obstructions had been placed in the river so that boats could not pass. The enemy had cut the levee on the Mississippi near, and the whole country was flooded with water. While here the boys learned that nearly every cypress tree in the swamp on the other side of the river was a bee tree, and they would cross over in boats, and lashing one on each side of it would proceed to cut it down, and being light they would float and then they would cut holes and let the water in drowning the bees, and then they would proceed to get the honey out. On the 21st the entire regiment went aboard the magnificent steamer *Magenta* and proceeded up the river to Rolling Fork, where we arrived on the 22nd. Co. A under command of Lieut. W. R. McGowen was left in support of a battery at Dr. Chaney's place, the remainder of the regiment advancing to meet the enemy under Sherman coming up Little Deer Creek with gun boats and a considerable force of infantry.[4] There was some skirmishing on this day and on the 25th, in which several men were wounded and John Yarborough of Co. C was killed. Our command was joined at this time by Featherstone's brigade composed of the 31st, 32nd, and 33rd Mississippi regiments, and an advance was made upon the enemy and they rapidly fell back.

The little stream in which they attempted to pass into the Yazoo River was so narrow that their gun boats could not turn around and they had to back out into Stule's [sic, *Steele*] Bayou, or Black's Bayou through which they had entered. While at Dr. Chaney's place at Rolling Fork it rained in torrents, and there being a large pile of lumber in the yard, the men made shelters to protect themselves but soon found that it was but little protection from such a rain fall. Lieut. McGowen, wiser than the rest of us, took possession of an abandoned negro cabin with a huge feather bed in it, and had a glorious night's rest, so he reported next morning.

On March 25th, the entire command camped at Indian Bayou, where we remained a few days under command of Brigadier General Fergurson.

On April 2nd, Companies A and B under command of Capt. E. D. Willett were ordered to Fish Lake, sixty miles up Deer Creek. At this time there was no more beautiful or fertile spot in the South. Large plantations highly improved with nice houses, cottages with two or three rooms nicely painted, laid out like a village in which the negroes lived, large barns and outhouses, gin houses and other buildings, all painted, with thousands of acres in cultivation, with the dark background of the forest in the distance formed a picture more beautiful than artist could paint. And on these plantations were thousands of bales of cotton and immense quantities of corn, together with vast number of cattle, hogs, horses, mules, chickens, geese, turkeys, in fact every thing to gladden the heart, stomach, I should rather say, of hungry soldiers. In one brief week this beautiful country was laid waste and nothing but blackened and charred ruins remained of what had so lately been so beautiful a picture. As we fell back we burned the cotton to keep it from falling into the hands of the enemy, and as they fell back they burned the corn, and all the buildings, and destroying everything they could to keep it from falling into the hands of the enemy. But this is anticipating. The first night we camped at the Willis place, the next at the Thomas place, the next at the Falls place and the next at Judge Yarger's [sic, *Yerger*] place, and from there we moved up to Fish Lake, where we reported to Maj. Bridges, who was in command of a battalion of sharp shooters. We had been here but a short time before it was learned that Gen'l Stule [sic, *Steele*] with thirteen regiments of infantry, eight pieces of artillery and two hundred and fifty cavalry, was advancing against us. This information came from a lady within the lines of the enemy and was sent by a trusted negro. We immediately broke camp and began to fall back and continued to do so until we reached the Thomas place where we met the remainder of our regiment and other troops, infantry and artillery hurrying up to our assistance. After some skirmishing the enemy fell back, pursued by our entire force, until we reached Greenville, where they were reinforced and we in turn fell back, but were pursued only a short distance, the enemy returning to Greenville, while we returned to the Helen Johnston place.

Stone's Battalion

Our Southern Home March 30, 1899

In my last article there were several typographical errors. The types made me say "Gen. Stule advanced, etc.," when it should have been "Gen. Steele." Also Stule's Bayou, or Steele's Bayou. Also "Judge Yarger" instead of "Judge Yerger."

On April 18th, the regiment went into camp at the Helen Johnston plantation on Deer Creek a short distance above Rolling Fork, after thirty days of hard service. In a few days there was considerable sickness in the regiment caused from exposure by wading in water, and lying on the damp ground. Several men belonging to different companies died and were buried on the top of some large Indian Mounds near by, among the number W. H. Harrison of Co. A.

On April 28th, Companies A, D, and I, under command of Major T. O. Stone were ordered up the Yazoo and Sunflower Rivers upon a scouting expedition, and to do picket duty. These three companies were thus separated from the regiment and being about one hundred miles up the Sunflower River when the enemy invested Vicksburg, were cut off and did not rejoin the regiment until just a few days before the battle of Lookout Mountain. It will be necessary to leave the regiment for the present and take up the story of the operations of these three companies known from that time until they rejoined their regiment as Stone's Battalion.[5] As stated we left camp at the Helen Johnston place April 28th, 1863, and took boat near Rolling Fork and ascended the Yazoo River some distance, stopping at Dr.

Hanna's Landing, where we remained a week or ten days spending the time eating, sleeping and fishing, when the buffalo gnats and mosquitoes would permit. There was some little hunting done too as there was considerable game in the swamp, deer, bears, etc. Lieutenants McGowen of Co. A and Vinson of Co. D went out on a "hunting expedition" one Sunday. It was "a poor way to serve the Lord" as one of them said, but soldiers in active service know but little difference between Sunday and any other day. After wading Dougherty Bayou and being gone nearly all day they returned, and reported that they had seen two "she bears" but did not see cubs with them; they both took a shot at the bears but with what results was not known, as they did not bring any "bear meat" into camp with them. Some of the boys doubted if they had ever seen a bear, and at most if they had seen anything that it was nothing more than two "bear skins." After spending a week or ten days at this place, for what purpose I never could ascertain, we took boat and proceeded up the Sunflower River until we reached a point about twelve miles below Friar's Point on the Bobo plantation. On this trip the boat had but little wood, so corn, which was piled up in great quantities at different landings, was used for fuel. We had been at the Bobo place but a few days when a steamboat came up the river with orders for us to return at once and rejoin our regiment. We learned that Grant had crossed the river below Vicksburg and that our regiment had been ordered to that place. We also had orders to stop at Rolling Fork and take aboard a number of men who had been left there sick and unable to accompany the regiment when it left for Vicksburg on May the 5th. When arrived at Rolling Fork we found quite a number who had been sick, in charge of Dr. Mays and several nurses. Among the number left behind and picked up by us was W. A. Altman of Co. C, now of York, who had remained to nurse a sick friend. He was then but a boy, having entered the army at the age of sixteen. He connected himself with Co. A and remained with us for five or six months and

34

I can truthfully say that no better or braver soldier could be found in the Confederate army, and what is worthy of all praise is that he was as modest as brave. We learned when we reached the Fort that Vicksburg had been invested, that Snyder's Bluff was in the hands of the enemy and that they were removing the obstructions at that place and that their gun boats might be expected up the Yazoo River at any time. So taking the men and baggage found there aboard, we immediately started back up the Sunflower River to give warning to a battalion of infantry under Major Bridges, a section of artillery and some cavalry that had been left behind. We stopped at Garvin's Ferry, where we remained a few days collecting the troops that I have mentioned. While here Capt. Gulley who had only recently recovered from a severe spell of pneumonia was taken sick and had to be left behind in charge of W. H. Webb, now of Cuba. Almost any one else in his state of health would have been at home, but his pride and indomitable will power kept him at his post of duty when his physical condition was such that he could scarcely walk. While Capts. Gulley and Webb were in their room a few nights after we left, hearing a noise in the yard Webb went to the window and looked out and saw that the yard was filled with Federal soldiers. Strange to say they did not come in, and Capt. Gulley and Webb escaped capture. This Federal force had been sent to capture our little command but we had two or three days start in the swamp. We pursued our way through the swamp from Garvin's Ferry on the Sunflower to Greenwood on the Yazoo, under great difficulties; the water had just gone down and the soil was soft and men and horses would flounder through as best they could. We frequently had to stop and unhitch the horses from the wagons and artillery and take them across the bad places by hand. We finally reached Greenwood and crossed just above Fort Pemberton. Scarcely had we crossed the river before the booming of the big guns from Fort Pemberton announced the approach of the enemy up the Yazoo River. They soon retired, however, and we had a quiet day of rest.

Our Southern Home April 6, 1899

I omitted to state in its proper connection that while the movements of our regiment, which I have narrated, were taking place along Deer Creek, it was deemed necessary to erect some fortifications at Rolling Fork, and there being no regular army engineer present, Capt. W. A. C. Jones, of Co. C, our present efficient Circuit Clerk, who was a practical civil engineer, was detailed to lay out the lines and superintend the erection of the fortifications, and so well was it done that it attracted the attention of the military authorities, which led to his transfer after the siege of Vicksburg, to the Engineer Corps where he was attached first to the staff of Maj. Gen. French and afterward to that of Lieut. Gen. A. P. Stewart and in this new field he performed valuable service. Capt. Jones always did his work well in what ever position he was placed.

Stone's Battalion remained at Greenwood a few days, resting and awaiting orders. About the middle of May we received orders to proceed across via Carrollton to Winona on the Miss. Central R. R. to a point opposite Yazoo City to join the force under Gen. Joseph E. Johnston that was being organized for relief of Gen. Pemberton. We reached Carrollton the first day and went into camp east of town. I had been quite unwell for several days and when the command moved the next morning I was too sick to march, so was left behind. I was kindly cared for by a Mr. Marshall whose wife and daughters could not have been more attentive to me had I been a near relative. As soon as I was able to do so, I proceeded to join my command which I did about May 20th, near Liverpool, Miss.

Our battalion was placed in Ector's Texas Brigade, which was part of Gen. W. H. T. Walker's Division, the other brigades being Gist's and Wilson's.

Gen. Johnston was making every effort to organize a force to relieve Vicksburg, but for weeks we could do nothing but lie idly by and listen to the roar of the artillery around Vicksburg, where our friends were cooped up and anxiously looking for us. But alas, we were helpless owing to want of transportation. An army without transportation is like a bird with clipped wings. Reinforcements had been hurried forward from Gen. Bragg's Army in Tenn. and Gen. Beauregard's in South Carolina, but the wagons and artillery came without teams to draw them, and they stood for weeks at the railroad, where they were taken off, while the county was scoured for horses, mules and even oxen to draw them. While we were thus idle, Gen. Walker, who was a rigid disciplinarian, issued an order that the troops in his division should drill eight hours a day, Sundays excepted. Ector's Brigade, to which we were attached, kicked against this and swore that they would not drill, that the weather was too hot and that they had been drilled enough to know how to whip the yankees anyway. So when the different regiments and battalions were marched out to drill, the last mother's son of them would lie down, and neither threats nor persuasions could move them, and after spending the required number of hours on the field they would return to camp. They made all sorts of fun of our battalion for obeying the order and drilling as required. They also poked fun at us for "packing," as they called it, our bayonets around with us, telling us that we would never get close enough to a Yankee to stick one with them, and that we had enough to "pack" without that extra weight, and it wasn't long before every bayonet had disappeared from our battalion. So much for demoralizing influences. Of all the harum scarum reckless fellows I met with during the war, these Texans were the wildest and most reckless. No braver men or officers could be found in the army, from Gen. Ector down to the humblest private in the ranks.

It was the 28th of June before the forward movement began. On that day, Loring's, French's and Walker's Divisions moved to

Birdsong's Ferry on Big Black River, while Breckenridge's Division was lower down near Edward's Depot. Our forces all total did not amount to much more than twenty thousand, while the enemy we were expected to attack, protecting Grant's rear, numbered fully thirty thousand behind strong entrenchments. Reconnaissances were made along the whole line, and the enemy found to be strongly entrenched. It would have been folly to attack at that point. So we moved down in the direction of Edward's Depot on the 3rd day of July, and Breckenridge's Division had pontoon bridges laid to cross over early on the morning of July 5th. But on the evening of the 4th, Gen. Johnston received intelligence of the surrender of Vicksburg, and we fell back to Jackson, where we arrived late on the afternoon of the 7th.[6] On the march from Big Black to Jackson, we suffered fearfully from the excessive heat and want of water. We marched through Jackson and bivouacked in an old field east of the city. So completely exhausted were the men by the long weary march that without waiting to eat, they threw themselves down on the warm earth and were soon fast asleep. A threatening cloud was approaching and soon a heavy rain fell, or I suppose it did, for when I woke I was thoroughly soaked and the water was running down the furrow in which I was lying to such an extent that my Confederate money in my pants pocket was reduced to a lump of pulp. On the 8th of July we took position in the works, little insignificant entrenchments, not more than knee deep. Walker's Division extended from the right to the Clinton Road along which the enemy was advancing, Ector's Brigade forming the left, and Loring's on our right. During the afternoon of the 8th the spattering fire of the skirmishers in our front told that the enemy was advancing. On the ridge just to our left was a battery commanding the Clinton Road. Connected with this battery was Sergeant Ball, whom we had first met at Deer Creek. Every member of Stone's Battalion will remember this daring and gallant soldier who was dangerously wounded a few days later, while serving one of the guns.

It was not long after we had taken our place in the entrenchments before the vicious zip, zip of the minnie balls told us that we were within range of the enemy's sharp-shooters. It is strange how soon one becomes accustomed to danger; when the bullets first commenced whistling over our heads almost every man would involuntarily dodge, and when a shell came hurtling through the air almost every man thought it was going to fall on the spot where he stood, but in a few hours men would walk about as coolly and unconcernedly as if the death dealing missiles were not flying through the air. The fire of the enemy increased in volume, extending along our entire front and intermingled with the rattling roar of small arms, the hoarse roar of artillery could be heard. We supposed of course that a heavy attack would soon be made, but we supposed their experience in charging entrenched lines at Vicksburg had taught them a lesson, as they refrained from doing so, and the fire subsided to a heavy skirmish along our front, but the artillery firing was kept up day and night.

It was a beautiful sight to watch the shells from the enemy's batteries with burning fuses pass overhead like sky-rockets and explode in the city and occasionally just outside our lines. Gen. Joseph E. Johnston was in command of the Confederate forces and Gen. W. T. Sherman, of the Federal. After we had been in line a day or two Gen. Johnston and staff passed along inspecting the works. Lewis Lancaster of Co. A stepped out and addressing Gen. Johnston, said: "General, do you think we can hold the works?" "I haven't the slightest apprehension," replied the General, pleasantly, and rode on.

It is not necessary for me to eulogize Gen. Johnston; he was every inch a soldier. Napoleon's "Old Guard" were not more devoted to their emperor than Gen. Johnston's men were to him. His men had the most unbounded confidence in his judgment, and no one doubted his bravery.

On the 11th and 12th the firing became heavier especially in our front near the Clinton Road. Clark Hitt was wounded in the hand, which had to be amputated, and Sim Baines was wounded in the shoulder. I omitted to state that Co. A was under command of Lieut. W. R. McGowen from the time we left Garvin's Ferry on the Sunflower River, until we had fallen back from Jackson, Capt. Gulley's continued ill health forcing him to go to the hospital where he remained a few weeks, and returned to the command after we reached Morton, Miss.

On the 13th our brigade—Ector's—was moved some few hundred yards to the right and Stone's Battalion was ordered out on the skirmish line. We occupied a skirt of woods some two hundred yards or perhaps more in front of our line of works. The ground in front was covered with undergrowth of bushes and it was impossible to see but a short distance in front. W. A. Altman and myself were together on the extreme right of our line with everything very quiet in our immediate front. All at once the blast of a bugle was heard followed by the command "Forward, guide center"—and we knew that a line of battle was moving forward against our thin skirmish line. Our men on the left commenced firing as soon as they heard the command to move forward, but Altman and I could see nothing to shoot at, so we held our fire. Altman was kneeling down behind a little hickory stump not larger than a man's wrist, when zip came a minnie ball just grazing the stump and not missing his head more than an inch or two. "By jucks," he said "that was a close call." In a few moments we saw the bushes shaking and both of us fired our guns, and some one in the enemy's lines cried out, "Oh, Lord." Whether he or I did it, I don't know, but the intention of each was to kill as many of them as possible. Our line of skirmishers fell back to the breast works and soon our batteries were pouring shells thick and fast in to the skirt of woods from which we had just been driven.

Breckinridge's Division held the extreme left of our line extending to the Pearl River. The rich bottom lands along the river were planted in corn, and at that season of the year was tall and very thick; the line of battle was across one of the these fields of corn, and as the Federal forces were advancing they came suddenly and to them unexpectedly upon Breckenridge's Division. The firing along the line at that point increased in volume until there was a continuous roll of small arms interspersed with the rapid detonations of artillery, which told that our lines were being assaulted in force. This heavy firing did not last over thirty minutes when a wild cheer—known as the rebel yell—went up from that part of the line, was taken up and carried around the circle of our entire line telling in unmistakable terms that the Federal assault had been repulsed. The Federal loss was very heavy considering the length of the engagement, while that of Breckenridge was small. In fact our loss during the fighting around Jackson was small, being only about six hundred killed and wounded.[7] It soon became apparent from the increase in the number of batteries and heavier lines of skirmishers that the enemy was concentrating the entire force at and near Jackson and it was only a question of time when we would be entirely surrounded. But Gen. Johnston was too shrewd to be caught in the same trap in which Pemberton had been caught in Vicksburg. So after sending off the sick and wounded to Meridian, and removing every article of value from Jackson, we proceeded to evacuate the place and fall back to Brandon. I don't suppose any of the old soldiers who were there will ever forget that night's march. We had been under fire in the trenches and in the skirmish lines seven or eight days, most of the time in the broiling sun without protection of any kind, and getting but little sleep, so one can well imagine how we stumbled along through the weary hours sleepy and tired. We reached Brandon about sun rise, where we rested a day or two—the enemy failing to pursue—we went into camp at Morton a small place on the Meridian and Jackson railroad, a few miles east of Brandon. Here we remained until the latter part of August, when our division (Walker's) and Breckenridge's Division were ordered to Chattanooga to reinforce Gen. Bragg, who was falling back into Georgia, just before the great battle of Chickamauga, which will be the subject of my next article.

"Just as Good as Texans"
Chickamauga Campaign

Our Southern Home April 27, 1899

August 22nd we received orders to hold ourselves in readiness to move at a moment's warning to reinforce Gen. Bragg at Chattanooga. The next day our brigade (Ector's) took the train for Meridian, where we remained twenty-four hours waiting for a boat to take us to Montgomery. At the latter place we had to wait about twenty-four hours for transportation to take us to Atlanta, where we again had to wait for sometime, thus taking about a week to cover a distance that can now be made in twelve hours. Such was the condition of the railroads that it was dangerous to run at a rapid rate of speed. As we passed through Alabama and Georgia the ladies in all the little towns turned out in great numbers to see the soldiers pass, and the boys would write their names and command to which they belonged on slips of paper and throw them out in the crowd, and in the course of a few days receive letters, but the girls took good care not to sign their names so the correspondence was one sided. I have spoken of the harum scarum character of these Texans. During this trip a great many of them were on flat cars and when there was a slack in the cars they would reach over and pull out the coupling pin and away the train would go, and run miles perhaps before the engineer would discover that his train was cut in two. In the mean time if there was an orchard near by they would rush out and fill their haversacks with fruit, and when the other part of the train would come back they

43

would make all sorts of fun at the engineer and yell out "Back up a car-length or two, Jackey." The engineers swore in their wrath that they never would haul that brigade again.

We reached Chattanooga after dark and ran into the city not knowing that it had been evacuated. Fortunately for us the enemy had not occupied it, so we quietly backed out, and stopped at Tyner's Station where we disembarked. After spending some time near this place doing picket duty, the army retired to Lafayette, Georgia, some twenty-eight or thirty miles from Chattanooga. Walker's Division together with Wathall's and Liddell's Brigades, under command of Gen. E. C. Wathall formed a demi-corps, under the immediate command of Gen. Walker. We understood that we were to act as a reserve for the corps of Gen. D. H. Hill in the impending battle, but if such was the intention the plan must have been changed, as we entered the fight early Saturday morning and were in the last charge Sunday evening.

While at Lafayette, Gen. Bragg had an opportunity that does not come to a general once in a dozen campaigns, of inflicting a blow that would have ruined Rosecran's Army. Two divisions of the enemy got into McLemores's Cove through a narrow gap, and were completely cut off from their main army by a mountain on one side and our entire army in their front, with our left wing as near or nearer to the gap through which they had passed, than they were. All that was necessary was to seize the gap and then overwhelm them with our army in front. Almost every soldier in the ranks knew the condition of affairs, and were sorely disappointed when our plans miscarried. As we understood it then—and I have never heard it contradicted— Gen. Hindman supported by Gen. Buckner with two divisions, was ordered to seize the gap, while Cleburne supported by our divisions was to press them in front. On the morning of the 11th we advanced and there was a lively skirmish in our front, but the enemy withdrew rapidly and their rear was just passing through the gap when Hindman's Division came into sight. We captured a few prisoners and ambulances, when we ought to have captured or destroyed the right wing of Rosecran's Army. We never knew whose fault it was. Gen. Bragg claimed that it was Hindman's and placed him under arrest, while Hindman insisted that the fault was Gen. Bragg's in giving orders and then countermanding them, and then renewing them until it was too late for him to reach the gap in time to prevent the escape of the enemy. We returned to Lafayette where we spent several days. In the meantime the enemy was concentrating in our front in the direction of Ringgold. We moved forward and formed line of battle hoping the enemy would attack us, but this he declined to do, and after remaining in line all day we were withdrawn to our original position. Bragg had been reinforced and it was known that Longstreet with two divisions of his corps from the army of Virginia was on his way to join us, and the men were eager for the conflict, which every private in the ranks knew to be inevitable in a few days, feeling confident that we would win the battle.[8]

On the morning of Sept. 17th Gen. Bragg issued his orders for battle and we began the forward movement which culminated in the great battle of Chickamauga, the most scientifically fought battle, in the opinion of eminent military men, fought during the civil war.[9]

Our Southern Home May 11, 1899

On September the 16th, General Bragg issued his famous battle orders, which sent a thrill through the army, and was received like those of Napoleon to his battle-scarred veterans, with wildest cheers. Although nearly thirty-six years have passed I can almost repeat it from memory. The following is a copy of the order:

Head-Quarters Army of Tenn.
In the Field, Lafayette, Ga.,
September 16th, 1863

45

"The troops will be held for an immediate move against the enemy. His demonstration on our flank has been thwarted and twice had he retired before us when offered battle. We must now force him to the issue. Soldiers, you are largely reinforced. You must now seek the contest. In so doing I know you will be content to suffer privations and encounter hardships. Heretofore you have never failed to respond to your general when he asked sacrifice at your hands. Relying on your gallantry and patriotism, he asks you to add the crowning glory to the wreath you wear. Our cause is in your keeping. Your enemy boasts that you are demoralized and retreating before him. Having accomplished your object in driving back his flank movements let us now turn on his main force and crush it in its fancied security. Your generals will lead you. You have but to respond to assure us a glorious victory over an insolent foe. I know what your responsibility will be. Trusting in God and the justice of our cause, and nerved by the love of dear ones at home, failure is impossible and victory must be ours."

BRAXTON BRAGG
Commanding Gen.

On the 17th we began the forward movement as indicated in the foregoing order. The soil around Lafayette is very light and when pulverized is like ashes. No rain had fallen for nearly twelve weeks and the passing of wagons, artillery, horses and men over the roads had ground them into dust two or three inches deep. As each division moved forward you could trace their line of march by the great clouds of dust that arose above them and the men were absolutely covered with dust—hair, beard, eyes and nostrils filled, so that they all looked alike. Our division (Walker's) was ordered to cross Chickamauga Creek at Alexander's Bridge. On the 18th we moved up in the direction of this bridge, and about the middle of the afternoon formed in line to support Walthall, who with his own brigade and that of Liddell was to force the bridge, the enemy being in possession, and holding it with a considerable force. Walthall's Brigade made a gallant charge and drove the enemy away, but the bridge had been so badly damaged that it was found impracticable for artillery to cross so that it became necessary for us to move further down to Byron's Ford where we waded the creek that night. Notwithstanding, the weather during the day was very hot and sultry, the nights were quite cool, and the water of the Chickamauga was ice cold. After crossing the creek we marched out a short distance, formed line of battle and lay down wrapped in our blankets. We had not been there long before a staff officer from Gen. Ector came to me and gave me an order to take my company to the front, where we were to do picket duty. While on picket line, Tom McGowen, a brother of Lieut. McGowen divided some peas he had managed to get and have cooked, with me. I had eaten the last morsel of my rations that day about noon, and with the exception of these peas, and some parched corn the next night, I had nothing to eat from Friday at noon until Sunday night after the battle was over. I was not aware while on picket duty that we were so close to the enemy. I found out next morning that we were not more than one hundred and fifty yards from them.

The battle of Chickamauga has been too often described for me to undertake anything more than an account of what took place in our immediate front, and the part taken in that great battle by the boys from Sumter. Indeed a private soldier or even an officer of the rank of Brigadier General knows very little of what is going on along a line of battle from four to six miles long, except as to that part where he is engaged.

Of the battle of Chickamauga Gen. Dabney H. Maury in a conversation with the writer a few years ago remarked that the battle of Chickamauga was the most scientifically fought battle of the Civil

War. In his book, *Recollections of a Virginian* he says—speaking of this battle: "It was the hardest stand-up fight ever made by the Confederate and Federal armies of the West. For two days the battle raged. At the close of the second day the Federal army was driven from the field in rout. Thomas alone held his division in hand, the rest in the confusion ran towards Chattanooga. Bragg's whole force numbered forty-six thousand men. When the battle ended eighteen thousand of them lay killed and wounded.[10] No army of modern war in the Old World or the New ever suffered such a loss and won the field." Mr. Davis in his book, *The Rise and Fall of the Confederacy*, puts the killed and wounded on the Confederate side at sixteen thousand. Even putting it at this figure it indicates that every third man went down, either killed or wounded, and when we consider that the Federal loss was as great or even greater we can form some idea of the courage on that desperately contested field.

On the morning of the 19th we were early in line waiting for orders to move and while standing on the road side, a part of Longstreet's Corps—two divisions about five thousand infantry without any artillery sent to our assistance from Virginia passed us on their way to take position on the left. They had on new uniforms of Confederate grey and moved like veterans and looked every inch the gallant soldiers which they were. In passing soldiers invariably asked, "What command is that?" So in answer to our inquiry we ascertained that among those passing was the 4th, 44th, and other Alabama regiments. They called out to us saying, "Boys, we have come down here to show you how to whip the Yankees." After the battle was over I heard some of them say that they didn't find it as easy a job as they thought they would have.[11] They overlooked the fact that a large part of Rosecran's Army was made up of Tennesseeans, Kentuckians and Missourians, and that among those from Illinois, Indiana and Ohio was a large percentage of descendants of the best blood of Virginia and Kentucky, as brave and courageous, as the bravest and best from the South. And towering above all was Gen. Geo. H. Thomas, a Virginian whose bull dog courage and pertinacity saved the Federal army from annihilation.

Our Southern Home May 18, 1899

We had but little time however, to exchange compliments with our Alabama friends as they passed, for about that time the heavy booming of cannon to our left interspersed with the spattering fire of small arms like the rain drops just before the thunder storm, and which soon deepened into a continuous roar, warned us that the grand overture to the battle had begun. Presently a staff officer dashed up, saluted Gen. Ector and directed him to lead his brigade forward at once to the support of Gen. Wilson. Gen. Ector gave the command forward, and we were soon pressing forward to the support of our friends who were so sorely pressed. On our way to the front we met a stream of wounded coming out. Some were hobbling along supported by some friend, others were holding shattered arms, and among the number I saw a fine looking officer sitting on his horse pressing his hand to his breast while the blood was trickling down his body and dropping on the ground. Another—an artillery man—had been shot through the face putting both eyes out, and his horse was quietly taking him to the rear. In addition to this, men wounded in every conceivable manner were being born out on litters, and along the road side the dead were lying, having been placed there by the litter bearers, who had picked them up on the field, and the poor fellows had died before reaching the field hospital. This might be considered demoralizing, but we had little time to reflect upon the horrors of war, for in a few minutes we were deployed in line, and advanced upon the enemy. This part of the battle field was undulating, not heavily timbered, with but little undergrowth. We had gone but a short distance before we discovered a heavy line of Federal infantry with several batteries just in our front. We had scarcely formed for the onset before they opened a murderous fire upon us, and we in turn upon them. The lines swayed backward and forth; we would drive them and then they would drive us. We were on the extreme right wing of our army connecting with Forrest's Cavalry on our right, and we were fighting Thomas' Corps, and that meant hard licks. Our loss in this brief struggle was terrific. Gen. Ector had his horse killed under him, and was himself wounded, but did not leave the field. Every member of his staff was wounded except one and he had his horse killed under him. Among the staff officers wounded was Capt. Kilgore, Assistant Adjutant General, afterwards in Congress from Texas, and known as Buck Kilgore. Every field officer except Lieut. Col. Dillard was wounded.

Stone's Battalion suffered heavily. Co. A lost E. G. Hammond and Jno. Dawkins mortally wounded. R. J. McGowen painfully wounded in the shoulder, Thos. Wildman badly wounded in the face, Elifus Ezell painfully wounded in the arm, J. A. Walker, Wm. S. Allison and several others slightly wounded.[12]

Col. Colquit, commanding Gist's Brigade, fell mortally wounded and his troops being under an enfilading fire, were forced to fall back. This left Wilson's Brigade exposed to the fire, and they fell back, and then Ector's. Upon reforming, our battalion connected with Forrest's Cavalry, and here I first saw the great cavalry leader. He was sitting on his horse just in front of his line of battle which extended as far as the eye could see, and I think he was the coolest looking man I ever saw. He seemed to be in a profound study, seemingly oblivious to the roar of battle and the scenes of carnage going on around him.

At this time the battle had been joined along the whole line—six miles, and the air was tremulous with the concussion of artillery. All along the line was one wild scene of death and destruction. The belching thunders of artillery, the exploding shells, the continuous roll of small arms, the clouds of smoke and dust, the wild cheers that arose above the din of battle, the groans of the wounded and dying, riderless horses galloping over the field, dismounted artillery, broken caissons, falling limbs and flying flags, brave officers leading their men, all combine to form a picture grand and sublime which no painter can depict nor describe.

The most desperate fighting had taken place on our right, the object being on our part, to turn the enemy's left and get between them and Chattanooga, their base of support. Of course their object was to defeat this if possible. Consequently Gen. Thomas early in the action on the morning of the 19th commenced calling for reinforcements and Rosecrans knowing the importance of holding this part of his line, promptly responded by sending men and guns as often as called for. We could tell by the increase in the number of guns brought to bear on our position that the line in our front was being strengthened. There must have been at least fifty pieces of artillery playing on us at once. Some six or eight hundred yards in our front, on a slight elevation the enemy had planted a battery of ten or twelve pieces. The fire from this battery was very destructive and our brigade was ordered by Gen. D. H. Hill to take it.[13] I shall never forget that moment. Gen. Ector though wounded rode out in front of his brigade, and gave the commands "Attention battalions. Shoulder arms. Right shoulder shift arms. Forward—guide center—March." These commands were given and executed just as if we had been on review. Forward we went, guns on the right shoulder, keeping step with the shells bursting, bullets whistling around us and men falling at every step. When we had gone about half way, high above the roar of battle we heard the commands, "Battalion halt. Lie down." This was done in order to give us a breathing spell before making the final rush for the battery. While lying here I saw something that was very amusing notwithstanding the serious surroundings. An old Irish man named Jimmie Barr who had joined Co. D of our battalion as a substitute was lying near me and was loading and shooting as fast as he could. I don't suppose he had ever fired a gun before. He would load, put his gun to his shoulder and when he would go to shoot, he would shut his eyes and turn his head away and in doing so he would elevate his gun to an angle of about forty five degrees, and then pull the trigger and bang away, and this he continued to do so as long as we lay there.

In a short time Gen. Ector rode out in front of our line, and taking off his cap called out in rapid succession, "Attention battalions—forward—charge." By the time the word "charge" had been uttered we were dashing forward yelling like demons. John Bunyard, of Co. A, while some twenty steps in front waving his hat and cheering his comrades on, fell pierced through the heart and died without a groan. No better or braver soldier fell on that blood-stained field than John Bunyard. A few minutes later Goodman Flowers received a painful wound in the groin. Several others were wounded whose names I cannot now recall.

On, on we went until within a short distance of the battery, and I thought surely that it was ours. I saw the gunners ramming home their loads. I knew that death and destruction was in that discharge, but there was no time to pause; one was as safe going forward as standing still. As soon as the gunners rammed their loads home, I saw them step aside, and then came the blinding, withering fire of the entire battery. The slaughter was fearful. The next morning I counted twenty seven of our brigade lying dead so near to each other that you could step from one to the other. They had gone down at one discharge like ripened grain before the sickle. When the smoke lifted we saw before us a long line of blue just behind the battery extending far beyond our flanks on each side. They had evidently been lying down until our near approach to the battery for we had seen no infantry as we approached. When we first discovered them they were in the act of firing, and we were soon met by a blinding sheet of flame and leaden hail. Our brigade already fearfully cut up by the morning's work, was unable to cope with this new and formidable force and there was nothing to do but fall back. I looked back over the ground we had traversed, covered with our dead and wounded, and it looked like a long, long distance to the point from which we had started, but there was no other alternative so back we went, bleeding, broken—almost annihilated. Ector's Brigade went into the fight that morning with about 550 men, and in the terrible struggle with Thomas, we lost 225 killed and wounded—being over 40 per cent of the entire command, and as I have stated Gen. Ector was himself wounded, and every member of his staff, save one, was wounded, and every field officer in the brigade but one was either killed or wounded. We venture the assertion that no more desperate fighting was done during the Civil War than was done by this brave little brigade. When we fell back the enemy threw out a heavy skirmish line, but did not advance their main line as they seemed content to hold what they had.

Our Southern Home May 25, 1899

We had a breathing spell after our failure to take the battery on the hill in front of us. We formed on the right of Cheatham's Division which had been sent to our support. It was astonishing how rapidly the men rallied and reformed, ready for another charge. It was now getting late; the sun was slowly sinking in the west—just above the tree tops. It sank so slowly that I thought some Joshua had commanded it to stand still. Wellington at Waterloo never wished more anxiously for night or Blucher, than I did for night or some command to take our place. The fact is I was tired. I thought we had done a good days work; the heat had been intense, and we had suffered greatly from thirst, there being no water nearer than Chickamauga Creek, a mile or more in our rear. The powder coming in contact with the lips in biting off the ends of the cartridges—for in those days we used Enfield and Springfield muzzle loading rifles—and inhaling the sulphurous fumes of smoke that hung over the field, aggravated the thirst caused by the heat and exercise. I was expecting every moment to hear the command "forward," when I heard in our rear the rattling of slate rocks, with which the field of battle was covered, and looking around I saw a sight that made my heart bound with joy. There, came a body of men that was to the Army of Tennessee, what the Old Guard was to Napoleon, or the Tenth Legion to Caesar. It was Cleburne's Division. On they came, tramp, tramp, tramp, every man keeping step, with guns at right shoulder, moving like a piece of machinery with their tattered, battle torn blue flags with a white crescent in the center, gaily fluttering in the breeze as far down the line as you could see.[14] We noticed where the water struck them above the knees where they had waded Chickamauga. They did not halt, but as they passed through our ranks, they said, "Boys, there are fifteen thousand men on the other side of the creek, who have not crossed yet." This was cheering news to us, for from the din and uproar that had been going on since early morn I had thought that every man we had within reach was engaged. Cleburne's men moved on with stern set faces, which plainly told that there was deadly work ahead. They had gone but a few hundred yards in our front before they were heavily engaged. It was indeed a grand sight, the grandest I witnessed during the entire war. This division single handedly and alone drove the enemy back—back, inch by inch, as it were, without cessation in the firing. Cleburne with his hard stern face was just behind his men, and they were too proud of him and their record to falter.[15] High over the roar of the battle you could hear their cheers as some battery was captured or position taken. Night coming on you could follow the course of the battle by the streams of flame that issued from the muzzles of the small arms, and the almost continuous flashes from the artillery like the lightning playing along the edge of a summer cloud, far in the distance. For over a mile Cleburne's men pressed the enemy back and held every foot of ground they had captured. Glorious old Cleburne, glorious old division! As long as heroism and bravery elicits the admiration of men, will their names live. McDonald's charge when he pierced the Austrian center at Wagram was not grander than Cleburne's charge at Chickamauga.[16] The ground traversed by Cleburne was covered with the dead and wounded, and all through the night the cries and shrieks of the wounded could be heard. Although it was but the 19th of September and the days had been excessively hot, there was a heavy frost that night, sufficient to kill tender vegetation, such as pea vines, potato vines, etc.

The wounded, weak and faint from loss of blood, suffered intensely from cold and thirst. We lay that night in line in the position we occupied when Cleburne's division passed us. I lay on a little rocky knoll, wrapped in a bloody blanket that I had picked up on the battle field—having lost my knapsack, blanket and everything I had, early in the action, and I felt very glad that I had not lost my life at the same time. Near by was a load of corn that had been emptied out on the ground and Tom McGowen and I sat up over a little flickering fire and parched corn and ate it, being all I had to eat except a hand ful of peas, since Friday at noon.

We had orders to attack the enemy at daylight, but it seemed that Gen. Polk who was in command of the right wing, failed to communicate the order to Gen. D. H. Hill, who was in command of Walker's and Walthall's Divisions. We remained in line from daylight until about 9 o'clock A. M., waiting for orders to move. All through the night we heard the enemy felling trees and we knew that the fight the next day would be against an enemy behind breastworks. About 9 o'clock on Sunday morning away down on our left Longstreet in command of that wing of the army with Stewart's, Johnson's, Hindman's, Preston's and his two divisions from the Army of Virginia (Hood's and McLaw's) opened the fight and it extended up to our front, when Breckenridge with his, a part of our division, took it up. The fighting was fierce, the brunt of it in our front falling on Breckenridge's division. It was Kentuckian against Kentuckian, and well did both sides sustain the reputation of their native State. We heard during the evening that Longstreet was driving them on the left, and sweeping everything before him. Everything was now being concentrated around Snodgrass Hill around which we had fought since early Saturday morning. Thomas was still holding on with bull dog tenacity. We were moved from the extreme right of our line further to the left, where a last determined effort was being made to dislodge him. As we were hurrying forward at a double quick, over the rocky slopes, the sun pouring down in rays with mid summer heat, drawing nearer and nearer to the place where the deadly struggle was taking place, and when it was evident that within a few minutes we would be engaged Tom McGowen who had been silently double quicking by my side, exclaimed "My God! I wish I could faint." I felt very much the same way, but as we couldn't faint, on we went, and in a few minutes afterwards we were deployed into line and moved forward. Gen. Ector was again wounded, and his horse was killed under him, but still he remained with his brigade.

As the sun sank to rest, one long wild cheer went up from the Confederate soldiers, and the battle of Chickamauga was won. Gen. Bate in speaking of this battle says; "The bloody field attested the sacrifice of many a noble spirit in the final struggle, the private soldier vying with the officers in deeds of high daring and distinguished courage. While the 'river of death' shall float its sluggish currents to the beautiful chant of its solemn dirges over their soldier graves, their names enshrined in the hearts of their countrymen, will be held in grateful remembrance as the companions and defenders of their country, who sealed their devotion with their blood on one of the most glorious battle fields of our revolution."

The storm of battle was over and the quiet that followed was as profound as the uproar had been great. We bivouacked that night on the field of battle. Most of the Confederate wounded had been removed, but the dead of both sides and a great many of the Federal wounded remained on the field. Our haversacks were empty, but those of the dead yankees were filled with bacon, crackers, coffee and sugar. We were hungry and these poor fellows had no further use for these articles. So while some of the boys went for water, others were making the fires and others were collecting rations from off the bodies of our late enemies. I don't think I ever enjoyed such a feast. In the first place I was very hungry and in the second place I felt glad that I had escaped without a scratch. Out of about forty belonging to Co. A who went into battle on the morning of the 19th only fourteen of us gathered around the fire that night.

After satisfying our hunger we proceeded about ten or eleven o'clock to take in the battle field. It was a beautiful night; the moon being nearly full, it was almost as bright as day. The dead were lying in almost every conceivable position; some lying where they had fallen looking as if they had fallen into a peaceful slumber while others with faces distorted indicated that they had died in great agony. Scattered around were knapsacks, broken guns, blankets and clothing and all the debris of a battle field. At one point where a battery had been stationed, I counted twelve large fine looking horses, lying dead, while near by were broken gun-carriages, trees shattered, the ground torn and blood stained, all going to show how desperate had been the struggle. Here was the reverse side of the picture, robbed of the "pomp and circumstance of glorious war." How many hearts had been made sad and desolate by these two days work? How many eyes grew dim waiting and watching for loved ones who never returned? How many a child would ask mother, "When will father come?" who was never more to know a father's love? In passing over the battle field we did all we could to relieve the wounded and make them as comfortable as possible, giving them water and replenishing the fires. Two wounded Federals were lying in a little field and seemed to be very comfortable considering their condition. While we were replenishing their fire, one of them—a little Irishman—said, "Boys as sure as that moon is shining in the heaven I never injured one of your wounded" and then pulling the blanket up and looking at his boot, which had been mashed into a jelly by a shell, he said "Och! I'll never dance on that again." Poor Pat, he is always ready for a fight or a frolic and it makes but little difference with him which—if any, giving the preference to the fight.

Our Southern Home June 8, 1899

The day after the battle was spent in burying the dead and collecting the small arms scattered over the field in immense numbers. Precious time was frittered away in this way when we should have been pressing the enemy. It is no excuse for a general, after he had driven the enemy from the field, to say that his men are exhausted and needed rest; the enemy is in the same condition, besides being disorganized and demoralized by defeat.[17] But this was too often the case with our generals, they seemed to be satisfied with driving the enemy from the field and rejoice over a fruitless victory.[18] The task of burying the dead was a hard one as we had but few spades and shovels, and the ground owing to the nature of the soil and the long continued drought, was very hard. Most of them were laid in ravines, and low places and a little dirt thrown over them. I saw the members of a Louisiana regiment burying one of their number—a mere lad—who had fallen in a little field in the last charge, and having no spades or other implements for digging a grave, they had with their bayonets hollowed out a place near where he fell, and wrapping him in his blanket they placed him in his shallow grave—his body being on a level with the top of the grave—and they piled the clods on him, scarcely concealing his body from view.

I noticed in going over the field that the Federal dead were much more swollen and blacker in the face than our men. There was a pallor about the face of our dead not seen on that of the enemy. Whether this was due to the difference of food or to the fact that the dead Federals had lain on the field longer than ours—as we buried our dead first—I cannot say. I also visited the hospitals filled with Federal wounded, I found most of them cheerful and quite talkative, and strange to say the bitterest enemies I found were Kentuckians.

On Tuesday morning our brigade received orders to be prepared to move that evening to Chickamauga Station to take the train to return at one to Mississippi to meet a threatened raid from Vicksburg. We left late in the afternoon and in about five days arrived in Meridian, coming by way of Mobile. The reins of discipline hung very loose upon the necks of the Texans. As we passed along at different points on our way, two, three and sometimes half a dozen men would step off the train and salute General Ector, and say, "General we will come on in a few days," and away they would go, and true to their word in a few days they would turn up ready for duty. We remained at Meridian about a week resting and taking things easy. Rumors of a raid from Vicksburg continuing, we were moved to Pelahatchie where our brigade was placed under command of Maj. Gen. French. As it was a standing rule of the Texans not to drill we spent the month of October very pleasantly, the only duty required of us being camp duty.

The other seven companies of the 40th Alabama having been exchanged after being in parole camp, at Demopolis for some time were ordered with the other troops at that place to Chattanooga to re-enforce Gen. Bragg's Army, when they arrived about the last of October, Maj. T. O. Stone, who had commanded the three companies known as Stone's Battalion up to and during the battle of Chickamauga, where he was wounded, being promoted to Lieut. Col., rejoined the 40th Ala. at Demopolis, and Capt. E. S. Gulley, senior captain of the regiment was promoted to the rank of major and took command of our battalion. On October the 30th, we received orders to rejoin our regiment at Lookout Mountain. We left the next day and reached our regiment about the 12th of Nov. We had been with Ector's brigade for nearly seven months, and with all their wild reckless ways had become very much attached to both officers and men—especially Gen. Ector and his staff.

When we first joined the brigade the Texans made all manner of sport of us—called us "Yellow hammers," "Mud turtles," etc., and never let an opportunity pass to tease and worry us—frequently asking if "our mothers knew we were out." But after the battle of Chickamauga all this changed—we had stood in line of battle with them, and had held our own, and from that time they looked upon us as being just as good as Texans. They became very much attached to us, so much so that the last night we spent with them they stole everything we had that they could lay hands on; cooking utensils, axes, rations—in fact everything that was worth taking. We had to leave early the next morning, so there was no time to investigate, and doubtless it would have done but little good if we had. This raid on us was purely in a spirit of mischief and fun. The next time we met them was in Georgia during the hard campaign of 1864, when they were marching to the music of minnie balls, and yet they yelled at us as they passed, "Hello boys, did you ever find your camp kettles?"

In looking over Col. Gulley's papers I find the following from Gen. Ector, of which every member of Stone's Battalion ought to feel proud, as indicating the esteem in which they were held by that gallant officer.

Head Quarters Ector's Brigade
Brandon, Miss., Oct. 30th, 1863.
"Major:—By direction of Brig. Gen. Ector, I send enclosed the order from Gen. French directing that your battalion report to its proper command. As a soldier he can but obey the order, but he de-

sires me to assure you that he parts with unfeigned regret from a band of men so gallant as those now under your command have proven themselves. Having been under his immediate notice in the great and glorious battle of Chickamauga, their conduct on that occasion was all that he could desire and elicits his warmest thanks. You have shared with us the monotony of camp, the privations of the march, and your actions on the blood stained field, any commander may well be proud of. Let all troops emulate your example and the blood of the haughty invader will soon enrich the soil which their footsteps now pollute. In conclusion he desires me to say that the connection, both official and private, with yourself and command has been most agreeable and in parting he hopes you will accept for them his best wishes for their welfare."

Very Respectfully,
T. B. Trezavant
Major E. S. Gulley, A. A. A. Gen. Comd'g Stone's Battalion.

VICKSBURG REVISITED

[continued from Our Southern Home June 8, 1899]

We now have the 40th Ala. reunited in a brigade composed of the 37th, 40th, and 42nd Ala. Regiments, under command of Brig. Gen. Jno. C. Moore stationed on the east side of Lookout Mountain.

It will be necessary to go back now to the time we parted from the regiment at Rolling Fork and trace their history up to the time when we rejoined them and in doing this I will have to rely almost entirely upon the diaries of Maj. E. D. Willett and Rev. Jno. H. Curry, of North Port, who was a sergeant in the company Maj. Willett took out from Pickens Co., and was also my Orderly sergeant when we surrendered in 1865. This, however, I will defer until the next issue as this article is sufficiently long.[19]

Our Southern Home June 15, 1899

[conflated by S. H. Sprott from the diaries of Maj. E. D. Willett and Rev. Jno. H. Curry]

May 5th, 1863, the seven companies remaining after the departure of Stone's battalion, were ordered to Vicksburg, and on May 7th took steamer for Hayne's Landing, where they arrived about night, and on the next day marched to Vicksburg, distant about fifteen miles, where they went into camp near the depot.

May 9th, were ordered to Fort Warrenton, ten miles below Vicksburg, and were placed in a brigade commanded by Brigadier

General John C. Moore, composed of the 37th, 40th and 42nd Alabama regiments and the 2nd Texas. The gunboats having passed the batteries at Vicksburg, they were concentrated near Fort Warrenton, which they shelled to such an extent that the regiment was moved back about a mile leaving only a picket line at the fort. On May 11th the entire regiment was on picket duty for twenty-four hours, Col. Higley, with one hundred men, occupying the fort while the remainder were held in reserve under command of Captain E. D. Willett senior captain present. The cannonading was terrific, but the men being well protected there were no casualties. The regiment remained here until the evening of May 15th, when they moved to within about three miles of Vicksburg. On the 16th began work digging rifle pits and cutting down timber in front, which was continued until late in the afternoon of the 17th, when the entire command was drawn back to Vicksburg. The battle of Baker's Creek had been fought and lost by Gen. Pemberton and he retired with his entire command, except Maj. Gen. Loring's Division which made its escape and joined Gen. Joseph E. Johnston near Canton, to Vicksburg, where Moore's Brigade with other troops went into the trenches, the 40th Alabama being on the left of the brigade and on the north side of the railroad.[20]

May 18th. The Federal forces advanced upon our lines; cannonading along the entire line and pressing the picket line.

May 19th. Heavy cannonading and brisk fighting early in the morning. Several men of the regiment were wounded and one man of Co.C killed. In the afternoon there was heavy fighting on the left, the enemy charging Herbert's Brigade but were repulsed with great loss.

On May 20th and 21st, the cannonading and picket firing continued without cessation.

May 22nd. The cannonading was terrific, the Mortar Fleet joining in the bombardment. About 11 o'clock A.M. the enemy made a furious attack along the whole line, but were repulsed with fearful loss.

At 2 o'clock P.M. on the 25th, a flag of truce was sent in by the enemy, asking permission to bury their dead and remove their wounded, some of whom had lain on the field, where they had fallen, for several days. During the time they were engaged in this the soldiers on the opposing sides met, talked kindly with each other, exchanging different articles and when the time was out retired to their respective lines, and again began the work of destruction.

May 27th. The Federal gunboat, *Cincinnati,* was sunk in front of Vicksburg by the Confederate batteries. The cannonading and picket firing continued day and night without intermission from May 27th all through the month of June. Our men were constantly on duty in the trenches exposed to the burning rays of the sun, and to add to the horror of the situation the rations began to fail. The corn was exhausted and peas were ground up for meal. The meat also was exhausted and mules were killed and eaten. The enemy kept drawing nearer and nearer, advancing their parallels until near enough to tunnel under our lines for the purpose of placing mines under them to blow them up. The only way to meet this was by counter mining, but notwithstanding the vigilance of our men one mine was exploded under the 3rd Louisiana regiment killing and wounding forty men.

The Confederate ranks were so reduced by sickness and the casualties of battle that the line of battle in the trenches was but a single rank and the men were two or three feet apart. Notwithstanding this the enemy did not dare to make another assault. Their experience on the 22nd of May had taught them to respect the thin line of weary, exhausted men in their front, and they preferred the surer but less dangerous course of starvation. The Confederates had been buoyed up with the hope that Gen. Johnston would be able to collect a sufficient force to break the lines of the enemy and bring them relief, but as days passed into weeks and weeks into months and no relief came every one saw that it was but a question of a few hours when they must surrender. There is nothing more galling to brave men, after all their suffering, privation and heroism, than to realize that all their sacrifices have been in vain, and that they must lay down their arms and surrender. But the time had come when this must be done.

On the morning of July 3rd., a flag of truce was sent out by Gen. Pemberton to ascertain upon what terms the surrender could be made. The terms being agreed upon, viz: that the officers were to retain their side arms and private property, all else in the way of arm and munitions of war to be surrendered—the entire force to be paroled and allowed to go home, and not to take up arms against the United States until exchanged—nothing remained to be done but to carry out the terms by stacking arms, and turning over all other public property, which was done on the 4th day of July.[21] Some have censured Gen. Pemberton for surrendering on this day, but it was inevitable, and it was useless to sacrifice more lives in a hopeless struggle, besides he perhaps obtained better terms than he could have done later. If censurable at all Gen. Pemberton was censurable for disobeying the orders of Gen. Johnston, his superior, in allowing himself and army to be cooped up in Vicksburg, where it was only a question of time when he would be forced to surrender. But it has been stated, whether true or not I do not know, that he had positive orders from President Davis to hold Vicksburg at all hazards. This I doubt, as Vicksburg had lost its importance when it had been demonstrated that not only gun boats, but the entire federal fleet could run the gauntlet of the Confederate batteries with but little loss and Mr. Davis knew too much about military affairs not to know this. Be this as it may, the fall of Vicksburg sounded the death knell of the Confederacy, and from that time on it was a hopeless struggle.[22] The siege of Vicksburg will stand out in history the equal of Saragossa or Sebastopol for the splendor of its defense.

SIEGE OF CHATTANOOGA

[continued from Our Southern Home June 15, 1899]

On July 11th, the paroles having been completed, the army of Vicksburg took up the line of march towards Enterprise, Miss., to which point it was directed, but in a few days it was found impossible to keep the command together, so when Gen. Pemberton arrived at that place he issued an order furloughing the men for thirty days, and ordering them to report at Demopolis, Ala. This was extended fifteen days, at which time they assembled at that place, where they remained about a month waiting for arms and other supplies. In the meantime they had been exchanged and about the last of October were ordered to Bragg's Army in front of Chattanooga, where they were joined by Stone's Battalion as heretofore stated, about the middle of November.[23]

Our Southern Home June 22, 1899

Moore's Brigade occupied the east side of Lookout Mountain, not far from the Craven House. Walthall's brigade occupied the western side of the mountain, picketing Chattanooga Creek from near where it emptied into the Tennessee River, up to the cliff of Lookout Mountain, while Moore's Brigade picketed along the creek to a point where it is crossed by the Memphis and Charleston R. R., thence down to the mouth of the creek being on the right of Walthall.

The forces on Lookout Mountain were commanded by Gen. B.

F. Cheatham, in whose division we had been placed. In a few days after Stone's Battalion had joined its regiment, we were ordered out on picket. Owing to the fact that the northern part of the mountain was exposed to a raking fire from a Federal battery at the point of Moccasin Bend, the moving of troops had to take place under cover of darkness, and one can well imagine the difficulties attending such a movement over the rough and rugged mountain side. I was in charge of a part of the picket line, and in visiting the different points along the line next day, what was my astonishment to find, sitting on a raft that extended entirely across the creek, about thirty or forty Federals and Confederate soldiers mingled together engaged in friendly conversation, and exchanging different articles. We were "short" in coffee and they were "short" in tobacco, so trade was brisk. I stood and watched the group for a few minutes, and heard one Federal soldier say, "Boys, if it was not for the politicians we would quit and go home and let you fellows alone." I learned that the two picket lines which were on opposite sides of the creek, and not more than twenty or thirty steps apart, had tacitly established a truce, and that they had promised not to fire upon each other without first giving notice, which was carried out in good faith by the Federals the day before Hooker advanced against Lookout Mountain.

Battle of Lookout Mountain

[continued from Our Southern Home June 22, 1899]

On Nov. 23rd, from our position on the mountain, we saw immense numbers of Federal soldiers—perhaps sixty or seventy thousand—in the valley in front of Chattanooga. Evidently,Gen. Bragg thought that he would be attacked in his front as only two small brigades—Moore's and Walthall's—were assigned the duty of holding Lookout Mountain against Hooker's entire corps, nearly ten thousand strong. But the massing of troops in front of Chattanooga was but a feint by Gen. Grant, and well it succeeded. Gen's. Moore and Walthall appealed day after day for reinforcements, but without avail. Again the two brigades were not in position to support each other.[24]

Nov. 24th was a cold disagreeable day, the mountain being enveloped in mist, which developed into a slow, steady rain fall, making it almost impossible to pass over the slippery rocks. We had been in line for some time, awaiting orders, not knowing that Walthall was engaged single handed with Hooker's entire corps. The fighting was done entirely with small arms, and owing to the condition of the atmosphere or the topography of the country, we did not hear the firing. Between 11 and 12 o'clock A.M. we were ordered forward to occupy some slight entrenchments that had been thrown up from the Craven House down the side of the mountain, but which were practicably worthless, as the entire line was exposed to a raking fire from the battery on Moccasin Point. However, we moved forward to occupy the line, and as we did so we found the enemy in possession of a part of it, whereupon that part of our line fell back, leaving several of our men and officers in the hands of the enemy, but in a few minutes order was restored and we made a rush for the works and recaptured not only the line of works, but also our men who had been for a short time prisoners in the hands of the enemy. Walthall's Brigade had been practicably destroyed before we knew it, and the remnant of his brigade passed to the rear as we moved to the front.

We held our position for sometime, repulsing the enemy handsomely several times, but General Moore finding that he was about to be flanked and that his brigade would share the fate of Walthall's, slowly retired to a point some two or three [sic, *hundred*] yards around the mountain, where he formed another line at a right angle to the one we had just left. Here we repulsed every effort made by the enemy to dislodge us. Finding that our ammunition was about exhausted, I sent Jack Roberts as we always called him, and as brave and gallant a soldier as ever marched to the tap of a drum, down the mountain to the ordnance train for a fresh supply; as he came back I saw that he was very much exhausted and ran to meet him to relieve him of his burden and distribute the ammunition. I had just taken the ammunition and turned to go back when I stepped on a slippery rock and went sliding down the mountain like a shot out of a shovel. It was done so quick that I didn't know "where I was at" until I came in contact with a large rock which stopped my further progress in that direction. About this time Gen. Pettus came up with his brigade and formed on our left. The fighting in a desultory way continued until after dark. This was the first time I ever saw Gen. Pettus on the battle-field and I was very much impressed with his soldierly appearance; he was cool and collected, and I heard him as I passed by giving orders for his men not to needlessly expose themselves. It is not strange that he won the love and confidence of his men; they knew that he was brave and fearless, yet he would not needlessly expose the meanest man in his brigade.

About midnight we retired from the mountain descending over a rough and rugged road, making our way to Missionary Ridge where we arrived about daylight on the morning of the 25th. Thus ended the so-called battle of Lookout Mountain or as the Federals delight to call it "The battle above the clouds." This affair did not rise to the dignity of a battle, in fact could scarcely be call a first class skirmish. I don't think the 50th [sic, *40th*] Ala. lost a man killed, and but a few wounded and a few captured on the picket line. This is not said in disparagement of Hooker's Corps, for it was a splendid body of men, and only a short time before had dislodged Longstreet's Corps from Raccoon Mountain, but it could not be called a battle when but two small Confederate brigades did the principal part of the fighting and they fighting in detail. A very small force could have held the mountain if properly handled and having a sufficient amount of ammunition, but both were wanting. Moore's Brigade, except Stone's

Battalion was armed with old smooth bore muskets. I know it is very easy to criticize, and in the light of past events, tell what ought to have been done, but it must have been apparent to the merest tyro in the art of war that with Lookout Mountain lost, there was nothing to prevent the enemy from pouring through the valley and turning our position on Missionary Ridge as they did the next day.

Missionary Ridge

Our Southern Home July 6, 1899

In my last article there were several errors that I wish to correct. The types make me say, "Gen. Moore finding that he was about to be flanked and that his brigade would share the fate of Walthall's, slowly retired to a point some two or three yards around the mountain, etc." which should read two or three hundred yards. Again the types make me say "I don't think the 50th Ala. lost a single man, etc.," when it should read the 40th Ala.

After descending from Lookout Mountain we crossed the valley reaching the southern end of Missionary Ridge about sunrise on the morning of the 25th. After resting for an hour or so we proceeded along the crest of the ridge, until we reached a point about the center of the line near Gen. Bragg's Head-quarters, where we had a fine view of the valley below, where the immense Federal hosts were formed in line of battle. Cheatham's Division belonged to Hardie's [sic, *Hardee's*] Corps to which also belonged Cleburne's, Stephenson's and Walker's Divisions, Cleburne was on the extreme right of our line while Cheatham was on the extreme left, Moore's Brigade being the left brigade of Hardie's [sic] Corps.

We had not been in position long before the fight opened on our right with a fierce attack by Sherman's Corps upon Cleburne's Division, but they met a fearful and bloody repulse at the hands of

Cleburne's men, leaving a large number of wounded and several flags in their possession.[25]

We were resting under the happy belief that we had gained a brilliant victory, and up to that time we had, but about the middle of the afternoon the Federal force in front of our center and to our left began to move; they came forward in fine style—great black masses, rolling forward like ocean waves. Our batteries opened upon them, the shells exploding in their ranks creating great gaps, but on they came. They soon carried Orchard Knob, occupied by our line of skirmishers. Here they halted for some time, as we supposed, to reform for an assault upon us in our immediate front, but they did not do so. It was now getting late and we supposed that the fighting for the day was over, but while we were feeling jubilant over our success, there came from our left and rear the zip, zip of minnie balls. Just before this Gen. Hindman passed along the line exhibiting the flags that had been captured from the enemy on our left [sic, *right*]. The minnie balls continued to come from our left and rear, and the news soon spread that the enemy was in our rear. One who has never experienced it, has no conception of the effect of the words, "the enemy is in our rear." Veterans who have faced fire on a hundred hard-fought fields, will become demoralized, and a few demoralized men can stampede a whole regiment. Gen. Cheatham came dashing down the line as fast as his horse could run, to see what the trouble was on our left. In a few minutes he returned at the same rapid speed and called out as he passed, "Boys, hold the line and I will have reinforcements here in fifteen minutes." But reinforcements could avail nothing so far as the left wing of the army was concerned; it had disappeared like frost before the morning sun.[26]

Gen. Moore with the eye of a practiced soldier, saw that some thing must be done at once to save our corps from the fate that had befallen our left wing, so the brigade was thrown perpendicular to our original line in order to stem the tide that was sweeping up the

71

valley behind Hardie's [sic] Corps, who all unconscious of the danger that threatened them, were rejoicing over the victory they had won.

After the enemy got possession of Orchard Knob, there was no further advance in our immediate front, but they held their position until our left flank was turned by a large force passing around the southern end of Missionary Ridge, by the same route we had that morning. So the first information our men on that end had, that there was an enemy near them, was a large force immediately in their rear. As soon as that part of our line gave way, the enemy poured in from the front and occupied our lines, and then commenced advancing along the ridge in connection with the force in the valley. It was at this juncture that Gen. Moore changed front so as to meet the enemy coming from this direction. The whole brigade—37th, 40th, and 42nd Alabama regiments—made a gallant charge driving the enemy back until a part of the works that had been abandoned were recaptured, but were finally compelled to fall back to the point from which they started, where they immediately reformed and charged again over the same ground, already strewn with our dead and wounded. We succeeded in checking the enemy and holding them in check until after dark when the army retired across Chickamauga Creek. Our brigade suffered heavily in these two charges. In Co. A, Wm. Irby and John Shelby were killed, and quite a number wounded. Among the wounded in the 40th Ala., was Capt. Thos. W. Coleman, of Co.F, who was shot through the body and reported mortally wounded, but with a splendid constitution and an iron will he pulled through and still lives, one of the most honored citizens of our state. Capt. Coleman was one of the officers who would never order his men to go where he was not willing to go himself, so when he fell he was in front cheering his men on.

Our brigade held its position until troops and artillery on our right got safely off and then about eleven o'clock we fell back in perfect order in the direction of Chickamauga Station. We lost in this fight over fifty pieces of artillery, and about eight thousand men killed, wounded and captured. The moral effect upon the army was worse than the loss of men and material. The men never did have that confidence in Gen. Bragg that an army ought to have in its commander. Only a short time before this a petition signed by nearly every general in his army, had been forwarded to President Davis, asking for a change of commanders, and stating that unless a change was made some great disaster would befall the army, but Mr. Davis had great confidence in Gen. Bragg and declined to remove him. This disaster was not the fault of the men, for they were the same men who had only a short time before fought so gallantly and heroically at Chickamauga, and subsequent to that time displayed unusual gallantry. It could with equal propriety be said that the stampede of the veterans under Early at Winchester, composed of such troops as Rodes' and Ramseur's divisions, was the fault of the men, but every one knows that this is not so. The young conscripts at Waterloo were not more demoralized or worse stampeded than the Old Guard, and the cry *"Sauve qui peut,"* was heard from the old grey beards, as well as the beardless recruits. My opinion is that these routs and stampedes result not from a want of bravery, but largely from fear of capture and a long uncertain captivity. If these men had felt satisfied that they would have been exchanged in a few days or a few weeks, they would have stood their ground and fought with the enemy all around them, but they knew that capture meant for them months, perhaps years of long weary captivity.

Our Southern Home July 20, 1899

Several errors crept into my last article, one of which was doubtless an error of mine. In speaking of the captured flags, I spoke of them as being captured on our left, when it should have been on our right. In speaking of the advance of the enemy, the types made me say "our battalion opened in fine style," when it should have been "our batteries." Again Gen. Hardee is put down as Gen. Hardie.

After our last charge Moore's Brigade fell back to its original position, reformed and awaited the advance of the enemy, but they were content to hold what they had gained, so they left us undisturbed. It soon became quite dark. Gen. Cheatham, riding by, inquired what troops we were and being told that it was Moore's Brigade, replied, "Boys, Moore's Brigade saved the Army of Tennessee tonight." Of course this was very gratifying to us, but we had done nothing more than any other body of troops would have done under similar circumstances, as we had warning of the approach of the enemy in time to keep from being stampeded, and when we were thrown into line perpendicular to our original position, we knew that there was no enemy in our rear and that none could get there without running over us from the front. After everything had been brought off safely from our right, we were ordered about nine o'clock to fall back to Chickamauga Station, where we arrived about eleven o'clock.[27]

Ringgold Gap

[continued from Our Southern Home July 20, 1899]

The next day we continued to fall back in the direction of Dalton. Late in the afternoon of the 27th we passed through Ringgold Gap and our brigade halted near a little stream that passed through the gap expecting to spend the night, but Gen. Hardee rode up and ordered us to move forward at once. We had not gone far when we heard the boom, boom of artillery and a crash of small arms.

To the right of the railroad coming south is a considerable mountain around the base of which flows a beautiful little stream, crossed by both the railroad and dirt road in the narrow valley dividing the mountain from a high range of hills on the opposite side. The railroad running north and south at this point runs parallel to one of these hills only a short distance away, and is perfectly straight for a considerable distance back in the direction of Ringgold, curving slightly just before it crosses the little stream, above referred to. Gen. Cleburne was protecting the rear with his division, and selected this place to give the enemy a staggering blow, that sent them reeling back in confusion. He placed his division along the crest of the ridge, which has been referred to as being parallel to the railroad, and which was covered with a thick growth of scrub oaks. At the curve in the railroad he placed a battery, covering it with pine brush.

Van Cleve's Division of the Federal army was leading the advance of the enemy, coming down the railroad in a dense column, laughing, talking, calling out, "Git Johnnie Reb," with guns slung carelessly over their shoulders, all unconscious of the danger that threatened them.

Gen. Cleburne was standing near the concealed battery watching the enemy as they advanced. Finally when they had reached the desired point, he quietly remarked to the captain in command of the battery, "Captain, you may open on them now." The brush were removed, and boom, boom, went the cannon and crash went the long roll of small arms as they poured a volley into the enemy in full length of their line. Not a shot had been fired by picket or vidette to give them warning, but like a clap of thunder out of clear sky came the awful crash of infantry and artillery. The slaughter was fearful—700 killed and wounded, 300 prisoners and three or four battle flags captured, was the result and all done in fifteen or twenty minutes.

The enemy, startled, shocked, and demoralized, disappeared from our rear, and Cleburne quietly withdrew his division across the little stream and bivouacked for the night. The enemy retired to Chattanooga, while we continued our way leisurely to Dalton, which place we reached the next day. We remained around Dalton until about the

8th of Dec. when our division—Cheatham's—moved about two miles southeast of Dalton, where wood and water were convenient. Here we went into winter quarters, and went to work clearing off ground and preparing to build cabins, and each company in our regiment soon had ten or twelve comfortable cabins, chinked and daubed so as to be almost air tight. This was the only time during the war that our regiment had the pleasure of remaining in winter quarters. The weather had been excessively cold since the first night after the battle of Missionary Ridge, and many of the men were but poorly provided with shoes, consequently suffered considerably in marching over the hard frozen, rocky roads.

WINTER QUARTERS 1863-64

Our Southern Home August 3, 1899

Shortly after we went into winter quarters, Brigadier General John C. Moore resigned, and Col. John H. Higley of the 40th Alabama being senior colonel present was placed in command and the brigade was known for some time as Higley's Brigade.

Soon after we went into winter quarters, Gen. Hardee, who was in command of the Army of Tennessee—Gen. Bragg having been relieved—began furloughing the men at liberal rate, those who had never had furloughs being preferred, each company being allowed one man. John D. Faulkner of Co. A was the lucky man from that company. John was little, black and ugly but was noted for being one of the best soldiers in the company, carrying the biggest knapsack, the biggest haversack, and the brightest gun in the company.

On January 1st, 1864, Gen Joseph E. Johnston took command of the Army of Tennessee. Gen. Johnston was the beau ideal of a soldier, and his very appearance won for him the love and confidence of his soldiers. The improved condition of the army was soon apparent. Rations were abundant, clothing and blankets were issued and the men were cheerful and contented. One of the first things Gen. Johnston did was to increase the number of furloughs, first two privates and one officer from each company, and then four privates. In addition to this each man who could obtain a recruit was allowed a furlough of twenty days. In this way many recruits were brought into the army, and the men returned cheered and encouraged by their trip home, and generally brought back large boxes of provisions for their friends from the home folks.

During the entire month of January the weather was excessively cold, so much so that there were no army movements. About the last of this month our brigade was ordered about five miles south of our camp to open up and repair roads leading to Dalton. After being out for nearly two weeks, we returned to our comfortable quarters, where we expected to spend the winter, but in about one week we were transferred to Gen. A. P. Stewart's Division taking the place of Strahl's Brigade of Tennesseans which took our place in Gen. Cheatham's Division. Stewart's Division was occupying the east side of Rockyface Mountain, where we were exposed to the cruel blast of the winter winds. Timber at that point was scarce, the cabins erected by Strahl's Brigade were small and uncomfortable since that brigade was much smaller than ours and our men were fearfully crowded.

Snowball Battle

[continued from Our Southern Home August 3, 1899]

After we moved to our new quarters we had quite a snow storm and the ground was covered with three or four inches of snow. Strahl's Brigade was attacked by a brigade of Breckenridge's Division, with snow balls and they soon called on the other brigades of our division for assistance and soon the divisions were engaged in a fierce battle with snow balls.

When we left our quarters each man took his haversack and as we went along they were filled with hard balls of snow, so that when we arrived upon the scene of action we were well supplied with ammunition. It was certainly a novel sight to see five or six thousand men engaged in snow balling. Bob Ferrel of Co. A, of the 40th Alabama in preparing one of his balls, by accident or otherwise, I am inclined to the opinion that it was otherwise, got a good sized piece of a brick mixed up with his snow and when he fired that particular ball at the enemy the result was that one of them fell as if he had been shot. Bob said when the fellow got up he saw the devil in his eye and thinking discretion the better part of valor he took to his heels and soon disappeared from the scene of action. I suppose he acted upon the theory that,

> "He who fights and runs away,
>
> Lives to fight another day."

About the latter part of January Col. Alpheus Baker, of the 54th Ala., was promoted to the rank of Brigadier and was assigned to the command of our brigade composed at that time of the 37th, 40th, and 42nd Ala. and later on before the campaign opened the 54th was added to it. Stewart's Division was at that time composed of Baker's and Clayton's Alabama brigades and Stoval's Georgia brigade.

The liberal system of furloughing adopted by Gen. Johnston together with a bountiful supply of rations and clothing had a happy effect upon the army. Absentees returned and recruits were constantly coming in so that a great many companies had almost their full quota of men. Everything betokened a desperate struggle during the next campaign, but the Army of Tennessee under the leadership of Jos. E. Johnston felt sanguine of success, and while others at that time may have despaired of success of the Southern Confederacy, it was not so with the soldiers in the field; they were the last to give up hope in the final success of the Southern cause and if the speculators and vampires at home had been as patriotic as the soldiers in the field the result might have been very different.

Comrades & Campfires

Our Southern Home *August 10, 1899*

Winter quarters! What memories cluster around these words? Is there an old soldier who does not remember the long winter evenings when he and his comrades sat around the campfire, and can't he now recall the features of each as they sat and whiled away the time in song and jest? Some of them still survive, but alas, "many a lusty form then present, was laid low ere the snow appeared upon the grass again." And many who spent the winter there passed through the war unscratched but since have answered their last roll call, "and have passed over the river and are now resting under the shade of the trees."

Often as I sit during the long winter nights gazing into the fire the face of first one and then another dear comrade rises up before me in imagination and thirty-five years are wiped out and I am a soldier again.

I can't undertake to give the names of all who were killed during the war or have died since, but can give the names of the officers. At that time the field officers were as follows: Colonel John H. Higley of Mobile; Lieutenant Colonel T. O. Stone of Pickens; Major E. S. Gulley of Sumter; Adjutant Clarence H. Ellerbee of Dallas; Geo. J. Colgin, Surgeon.

Of these Col. Higley and Major Gulley, who afterwards became lieutenant colonel, passed through the war safely and died only a few years ago. Lieut. Col. Stone was taken sick the later part of April 1864, and died on May 5th of pneumonia. Col. Higley and I sat up with him the night he died and he was bright and cheerful, conversing with me until a few minutes before he died. We had been intimately associated during the campaign of 1863, and had become very much attached to each other and just before he died he was planning for my future. He was a warm hearted accomplished gentleman.

Adjutant Ellerbee passed through the hard campaign of 1864 unscathed only to fall in the last battle in which the Army of Tennessee was engaged at Bentonville, N.C. No braver or more knightly gentleman laid down his life for the Southern cause than Clarence H.

Ellerbee. The surgeon of the regiment, Dr. George J. Colgin of Sumter, survived the war and died in Louisiana. The assistant surgeon, Dr. Hutchinson of Mississippi, I have lost sight of. Of the officers of Co. A then present Capt. James Cobbs is dead. Of Co. B Capt.—afterwards—Maj. E. D. Willett died only a few years ago. Lieut. James A. Latham, who became captain when Major Willett was promoted—was killed at Bentonville March 19th, 1865. He and Adjutant Ellerbee were both struck in the forehead by a minnie ball. Capt. Latham fell inside the federal breast works which we had just captured. I placed his blanket under his head and left him where he fell. Brave, gallant Latham deserved a better fate. Lieut. J. H. Wier died after the war, and also Lieut.Thomas. Lieut. E. D. Vance was killed July 28th at the battle of Peachtree Creek near Atlanta. Of Co. C, Capt. T. M. Brunson, Lieut. J. W. Monette, Lieut. N. E. Thomas and Lieut. James G. Hartsfield all died after the war. Of Co. D, Capt. A. G. Campbell, Lieut. V. R. Williams and Lieut. Thomas Vinson died after the war.

Of Co. E, Captain Ed. Marsh was killed May 10th, 1864 on Rockyface Mountain. Gallant, impulsive Ed. Marsh! No better soldier than he fell fighting for his country's cause. Lieut. E. Ward was killed after the war.

Of Co. F, Lieut. J. H. Knighton died several years after the war. I will say right here that in my judgment, Lieut. Knighton and Lieut. J. W. Monette were the coolest men in battle I ever saw. Of all the officers in the 40th Ala. they had perhaps the best reputations for cool deliberate bravery.

I am not advised as to who among the officers of Co. G—if any—have died; none of them were killed during the war, tho' Lieut. Powell Baker was badly wounded, losing a leg at the battle of Peachtree Creek. Of Co. H, Capt. C. C. Crowe and Lieut. Howell have both died since the war. Co. I being from Covington County, I have not been able to ascertain who among the officers in his company, if any, have died.

Of Co. K, Capt. A. M. Moore and Lieut. B. B. Sanders have both died within the past few years. Thus we see just taking the officers alone, what a large percentage of them have passed away since they were camped along the brow of Rockyface Mountain during the winter of 1864, and it is reasonable to suppose that the same, if not a greater percentage of the privates and noncommissioned officers have in like manner passed away.

The duties of camp were not onerous; the general health good; and in turn nearly every one had an opportunity of visiting home during the winter and came back cheerful and happy. Songs were sung, most of them now out of date, but at that time new and popular. Who does not remember "When This Cruel War is Over," or "Lorena," or "Tis Years Since Last We Met." Ah me! Our hearts were young then and most of us had a girl at home, blue eyed, black eyed, brown eyed or hazel eyed, but it made no difference about the color of her eyes, each had a strong manly heart whose pulsations were quickened as he thought of her or heard her name mentioned. But alas! Many a brave heart filled with the love of some dear girl at home, had ceased to beat before the frost of another winter appeared.

Revival

[continued from Our Southern Home August 10, 1899]

During the winter of 63-64 a most wonderful revival occurred in the Army of Tennessee. Rev. J. P. McMullen a Presbyterian minister from Pleasant Ridge in Green County—of whom I will have something to say in the future—came to our brigade, as a volunteer chaplain and stopped with Col. T. C. Lanier who was in command of the 42nd Ala., who was an elder in one of his churches. He had not been with us long before he and the chaplains of the different regiments inaugurated a regular protracted meeting; they had preaching every night and the men turned out voluntarily in large numbers, and seemed to be deeply interested. It was grand to hear from five hundred to a thousand strong male voices joining in "Jesus Lover of my Soul," or "Rock of Ages." A large number were converted and joined the different churches. There was no undue excitement, and nothing done or said—as is sometimes the case upon revival occasions, for effect, but every thing was calmly and deliberately done by serious men intent on serious business. This revival was not confined to our brigade or division but pervaded the entire army.

Deserters Shot

[continued from Our Southern Home August 10, 1899]

After the battle of Missionary Ridge there was a considerable number of desertions from the army principally from North East Alabama and North Georgia. After we were settled in winter quarters quite a number of these deserters were arrested and brought back, tried by court martial and sentenced to be shot and among the number two from our division belonging to Stovall's Brigade.

Their execution was one of the saddest scenes I ever witnessed. It was the latter part of April and the trees were just beginning to put on a tinge of green that indicated the approach of spring; the sun was shining brightly, the birds singing sweetly, everything indicating a return of life and vigor when two men, one of them at least forty years of age, were slowly marched around our division which formed three sides of a hollow square. Just in front of them were their coffins borne by four men each, and in front and rear of them the provost guard, all preceded by a brass band playing the dead march. Of all the sad wailing sounds I ever heard that was the saddest as it went floating over hill and valley.

As the prisoners passed Stovall's Brigade to which they belonged, they were allowed to shake hands with their friends and then pass on with tears streaming down their faces. When they reached the center of the vacant side of the square they were seated on their coffins, and at the command of the captain of the Provost Guard a volley was fired, and all was over. The division was marched by the place of execution in order that each man might witness the fate of the deserter.

Twenty-seven men were sentenced to be shot on that day, and twenty-five of them were executed in different parts of the army. Two of those sentenced to death were brothers and belonged to an Alabama regiment. When they were marched out and placed in position to be shot, an officer stepped forward and read an order from Gen. Johnston granting a full pardon for the reason that they had a brother in the same regiment who was one of the bravest and most gallant men in it, and his petition for their pardon was signed by the officers of the regiment, who spoke in the highest terms of his bravery and gallantry. If these men, snatched as it were from the very jaws of death, did not make good soldiers after that they were very poor material and it is a pity they were not shot.

Tunnel Hill

Our Southern Home August 24, 1899

About the middle of February, 1864, General Sherman advanced from Vicksburg in the direction of Meridian, Miss., with an army of thirty-five thousand men. General Polk who was in command of this department called on Gen. Johnston for reinforcements, and the divisions of Gens. Cheatham and Cleburne under Lieut. Gen. Hardee, were hurried off to Gen. Polk's assistance. Before they arrived, however, the enemy retired and they returned to the Army of Tennessee. In order to prevent Gen. Johnston from reinforcing the army under

Gen. Polk, Gen. Grant ordered a large force under Gen. Thomas to advance against our forces at and near Dalton. On the morning of Feb. 23rd the booming of cannon was heard in the direction of Tunnel Hill and soon the long roll was heard on all sides and men were seen hurrying from all directions, seizing their guns, buckling on their cartridge boxes, putting on haversacks and blankets, and in a few minutes the regiment was formed, and in like manner the brigade and then the division and in thirty minutes the heads of different columns could be seen advancing along the valleys and edges of the mountain to take their respective places in line of battle. In addition to the great lines of infantry winding around through the valleys and up the side of Rockyface Mountain, the batteries belonging to the different commands were rushing forward to take their positions in the line. It is wonderful what a perfect piece of machinery a well organized army becomes. In less than one hour from the beating of the long roll which was the signal for every man to fall in line, the entire army was in line to receive the enemy. I will remark here that an old soldier who has once heard the long roll will never forget it; it has a startling effect; the most sluggish and stupid man in the ranks will respond to the rat-a-tat-ta-tat coming in unending streams and gathering force and strength as it comes rolling from the drum.

Our division—Stewart's—occupied the right of our line, our left resting on Mill Creek Gap. Through this gap, which was quite narrow at this point, both the railroad and dirt road leading in the direction of Tunnel Hill passed. We had not been in position long before we could see coming down the valley in our front long lines of wagons, and ambulances and then artillery all moving leisurely in our direction. These were the wagons and artillery belonging to Wheeler's Cavalry and was being sent to the rear to be out of the way which indicated that the enemy was advancing in force. Wheeler retired slowly before the enemy and it was late in the afternoon before his cavalry began to pass through the gap. I was standing near the road over which they were passing, and some half and hour or more after the troops as I supposed, had all passed, I looked up the valley and I saw a lone horseman coming down the road at a break-neck speed leaning forward and using his old wool hat for a whip and bringing it down with a tremendous thud on his horse's flank at every jump. He never drew rein until safely within our lines when he suddenly stopped looked back up the valley drew a long breath and said "now d—n you, you will stop I reckon." He evidently thought that the entire Federal army was devoting its entire attention to him and he didn't feel safe until behind the solid lines of infantry reaching away as far as eye could see to the right and left of the gap.

On the morning of the 25th the fighting was general along the whole line; the enemy being handsomely repulsed in every charge. Clayton's Alabama brigade was detached from our division and placed under Gen. Hindman on our extreme right to guard Crow Valley. Late in the afternoon we heard heavy and continuous firing in that direction which finally subsided and we heard the rebel yell, which told us as plainly as words could, that we were victorious. In a few minutes the news passes down the line that the enemy had been repulsed with fearful slaughter. The brunt of the battle fell upon Clayton's Brigade and though attacked by overwhelming numbers they held their ground. Knowing that to them was entrusted the fate of the army, for if the enemy had succeeded in gaining an entrance into Crow Valley they would have been in the rear of the right wing of our army and the story of Missionary Ridge would have been repeated . While this was taking place on our right, our line was subjected to a severe artillery fire which we knew was preparatory to a charge which was made late in the afternoon. The enemy advanced boldly into the mouth of the gap but a well directed fire from the two brigades of our division present—Baker's and Stovall's and a concentrated artillery fire soon drove them back in confusion. During the artillery fire from the enemy we were lying behind our line of slight earthworks. Lewis Lancaster, of Co. A, becoming tired of lying in a cramped position concluded that he would get out behind a stump near by and stretch out and rest himself. The soil on that part of our line was full of gravel and as a shell would come over and about the time it would explode I would throw a handful of pebbles against the stump. This was not repeated more than two or three times before Lewis came tumbling into the trench swearing that the fragments of the shell hit the stump behind which he was lying every time they fired. The laugh was on Lewis but he took it good naturedly.

The assault on our division was the last serious attempt made by the enemy on our lines. During the night they retired, and the next morning we pursued them as far as Tunnel Hill, where it was ascertained that they had gone back to Chattanooga, so we returned to our former quarters.

General Johnston's management of this affair increased the admiration of his soldiers for him, and his presence upon the field inspired the men with confidence. At this time General John B. Hood, who had been made a lieutenant general, joined us and the Army of Tennessee, was divided into two corps, one under Lieutenant General Hardee, and the other under Lieut. Gen. Hood. Our division, together with Stevenson's, Bates,—formerly Breckenridge's—and Hindman's constituted Hood's Corps. While Hardee's Corps was composed of the divisions of Cheatham, Cleburne, Walker and Anderson.

When we returned to our quarters we fell into the usual routine of camp life. Several hours each day were spent in drilling, and performing other camp duties. Owing to continued ill-health, Lieut. W. R. McGowen, of Co. A, resigned, and W. Y. Peteet, of the 9th Mississippi—a Sumter County boy—was elected 3rd Lieutenant, and transferred to our regiment. Capt. Cobbs, being absent on sick leave, I was in command of Co. A during the campaign of 1864. Our regiment at the opening of the campaign of '64, was in splendid condition and recruited up to nearly its full strength.

87

THE ATLANTA CAMPAIGN

Our Southern Home August 31, 1899

As stated, after the enemy retired from our front at Rockyface Mountain we returned to our winter quarters and the months of March and April were spent in drilling, reviews and picket duty. We were well clothed and rations were abundant and good, and the morale of the army was never better. Different commands of infantry and artillery were scattered about, and the silvery notes of the bugles as they sounded the reveille and tattoo, and different calls, could be heard on all sides.

We anticipated an early advance of the enemy, but April passed away without any indication of an advance on their part. General Sherman was preparing to advance with an overwhelming force, and was taking his time to prepare thoroughly. General Johnson has been censured by some, most of whom never smelt gunpowder on the battle field, for not attacking Gen. Sherman and bringing on a general engagement. These critics know nothing about the true condition of things. The entire force under General Johnston amounted in all to forty-two thousand eight hundred and fifty-six men. Gen. Sherman's Army which had been largely reinforced amounted all told, to about sixty-five thousand men, and this disparity of forces continued throughout the campaign. Even if Gen. Johnston had attacked the enemy and defeated him, he was near his base at Chattanooga which had been strongly fortified, and the victory, like Chickamauga, would have been a barren one. On the other hand, if we had been defeated we would have been a hundred miles from our base at Atlanta with several rivers to cross.

The campaign of 1864 from Dalton to Atlanta will stand in history as one of the hardest and best conducted in the annals of military operations. Those of us who were in that campaign know what it was; for more than seventy days, fighting almost every day, marching through mud and water day and night the fight went on. Gen. Sherman could move up in our front, fortify and then throw a force equal to ours on the right or left flank and thus force us to change our positions to meet these movements.[28] So it was day after day and night after night the fight went on, and even in sleep the din and roar could be heard. Often when the firing would increase so as to indicate that perhaps a charge was about to be made, the difference in the firing would be noted in my sleep and I would jump up giving the command "fall in," and the men would promptly form in line. Gen. Hardee, who commanded one of the corps of the Army of Tennessee, stated that we inflicted a loss upon the enemy—from the opening of the campaign at Dalton until the 18th of July, the day Gen. Johnston was relieved—in killed, wounded and captured a number equal to our whole army.

On May 5th everything indicated an early advance of the enemy. Wagons were loaded and everything made ready to move when necessary. Rockyface Mountain had been well fortified and we felt confident of holding it against any number of men attacking from the front. Our division took position to the left of Mill Creek Gap, Baker's Brigade on the left of the division, the 54th Ala.—Gen. Baker's old regiment—under Col. Minter, joined us, with this addition our brigade numbered about two thousand effective men.

The enemy not appearing in our front we returned to our quarters, where we cooked three days rations and next morning returned to our place on the mountain. Nothing of importance occurred on the 6th, the fighting in our front in the direction of Tunnel Hill being between the advance forces of the enemy and our cavalry under General Wheeler. On the 7th our cavalry was driven in, the enemy advanced and the campaign of 1864 was opened. Our division—Stewart's—was advanced to support our cavalry and went as far as Burnt Bridge and from there to a range of hills where we remained until 12 o'clock at night, when we fell back to our original position. On the morning of the 8th, companies A, B, C, D, G, and I of the 40th Ala., under Capt. E. D. Willett, were thrown out as skirmishers, and had a skirmish with the enemy, driving them back across the creek. We lost several men killed and wounded, among them a young boy belonging to Co. C, whose name I cannot now recall, who had only been with us a few weeks.

On the 9th our division was relieved by Bate's Division, and we took our position on the opposite side of the gap, being the same we had occupied in February. On the 10th and the 11th the fighting was continuous along the whole line—every assault of the enemy being handsomely repulsed. About daylight on the morning of the 12th the 40th Ala. regiment relieved the 37th and 42nd Ala. on the skirmish line, companies A, B, and I occupying the redoubts, the other companies being held in reserve. A very heavy rain had fallen the night before and the men of the 37th and 42nd just as they were leaving the line concluded to unload their wet guns, and turned them loose in the direction of the enemy. This drew a heavy fire from the enemy, under which we had to go into the redoubts. Co. A sustained no loss but Cos. B and I suffered heavily in killed and wounded. The companies in reserve also suffered severely—Capt. Ed. Marsh of Co. E being killed while dressing his company. Lieut. John C. Moore of Co. H was also severely wounded. The fight was continued throughout the day and repeated charges made, but we were able to hold the line without calling upon the reserve for assistance.

On the morning of the 13th we were relieved by Stoval's Brigade, and resumed our position on the main line, where we remained until 12 o'clock that night, when we were ordered to move at once in the direction of Resaca, it having been ascertained that the enemy failing in their attempt in our front, were passing through Snake Creek Gap.

We had been in the skirmish line all through the night the night before, and when relieved had taken our place in line of battle, so we had had but little, if any sleep. Those who know anything about the movements of a large army, know how tiresome it is at any time. A column will be moving forward and perhaps another body of troops will be moving along or across the same line, then it is a halt, standing still for a few minutes, then move up a few steps and stop, and after a considerable time move up a few more steps and this continues for perhaps an hour. During one of these halts I leaned over and rested my head on the shoulder of the Orderly Sergeant T. T. Donald and when I awoke I was moving along with the sergeant. I don't think I have ever before or since been so sleepy as I was that night.

Battle of Resaca

Our Southern Home September 7, 1899

We took position in front of Resaca on the 14th, our line extending entirely around that place from a point a mile or more above on the Oostanaula River to a point a short distance below the railroad bridge. Hood's Corps was on the extreme right, Gen'l Polk, who had joined us with a part of his force from Mississippi, occupied the extreme left, and Gen. Hardee's Corps occupied the center. During the morning of the 14th the fighting was heavy and continuous on the left and left center. Stewart's Division held the extreme right of our line of battle. Just in front of us, some two or three hundred yards, was a large handsome residence in a beautiful grove of oaks. If the enemy should get possession of this, it would enable them to enfilade our lines and annoy us very much. So we were ordered to burn it. Most of the furniture was removed, and among other things a fine piano, which was placed under the shade of one of the large oaks. Gen. Baker, who had quite a talent for music and could perform passably well, sat down and played and sang. It was a scene never to be forgotten; the burning building, the booming cannons, bursting shells and continuous roll of small arms, all combined to form a picture, perfectly awful in its grandeur.[29] Our hospital had been established across the river, and in the rear of our wing of the army. Our servant, Martin Swann—the slave of S. D. Swann, of my company—had been sent there to take care of our baggage and cook our rations. Some Federal cavalry had crossed the river some distance above and very unexpectedly dashed into the hospital camp. There was a stampede among the surgeons, nurses and servants. Our boy Martin, with my baggage and his master's, swam the river, but landing at a point where the shells were falling thick and fast and concluding that he had "jump from the frying pan into the fire," he immediately swam back to the other side, and the next time we heard from him he was at York Station in this county, still holding on to our baggage. When he got home he reported that "de yankees done killed all our folks."

When the Federal cavalry made their dash into our hospitals, Gen. Wheeler happened, fortunately for us, to be near by, and before they had time to do any damage Wheeler was upon them, routing them completely. Late in the afternoon our division was moved to the front near the railroad, from which point we were, in connection with Stevenson's Division, to make an attack upon the left of the enemy. As we entered the fight we were to make a half change of front. I remember Gen. Stewart riding up and pointing out the direction he wanted us to take. Our division being on the right had to move much more rapidly than that of Stephenson—his left being the pivot upon which we turned. I never saw a prettier movement executed on the battlefield. Capt. Willet, of the 40th Alabama was in command of the skirmishers covering Baker's Brigade. After passing a skirt of woods near the railroad we entered an old field where we executed the change in direction, the skirmish line being warmly engaged in our immediate front. The movement was beautifully executed, the entire division could be seen, the enemy retiring rapidly in our front, the flags floating along the whole line, the men moving like a piece of machinery. It was an inspiring sight. Rev. J. P. McMullen, the volunteer chaplain of whom I have spoken, and who had a son in the 42nd, was following that regiment riding a little mule. When the 42nd moved out quite a number of the men threw their blankets in front of him on his mule so that he had quite a pile. When we were moving across the old field and were driving the enemy before us like a flock of sheep, the old gentleman became so excited that he rushed out in front on his little mule with his pile of blankets in front of him and taking off his hat led the charge. His long grey hair and beard gave him a venerable appearance, and rushing out as he did, when the men were already full of excitement and enthusiasm, Gen. Johnston himself leading a charge would not have been more heartily cheered. After driving the enemy about a mile and a half and it being now quite dark, we were halted and our lines readjusted. We were then withdrawn to the position we had occupied in the morning. Our loss in this charge was not very heavy. Henry Harris of Co. A, was mortally wounded, and others may have been slightly wounded though I cannot now recall any, nor do I now remember the names of any from Co. C or K killed or wounded.

After we retired the enemy moved up to the edge of the skirt of woods just west of the railroad. We could hear batteries being placed in position and the sound of axes cutting down timber and driving stakes, all of which indicated that the enemy had moved up in our front and were fortifying their position, and further that if we attacked them it would be at a fearful disadvantage. About 5 o'clock in the afternoon of the 15th our division was again moved forward in the direction of the railroad. The 37th Ala. was on our right and the

42nd and 54th on our left. Just to the left of our brigade was Clayton's Brigade composed of the 18th, 36th, and 38th Alabama regiments. On the right of our division there was no support, though Maney's Brigade moved in about the time our division retired. We had not crossed the railroad but a few minutes before we were under fire. We continued to advance until within 30 yards of the breast works, but the slaughter was so great that it was found impossible to proceed and the order was given to fall back. Col. Lankford of the 38th Alabama, just to our left not only reached the works but went over with the flag of his regiment in one hand and his sword in the other. Several guns were leveled at him, but a Federal officer gave the order not to shoot so brave a man. Rev. Mr. McMullen, as on the evening before, went in just behind the 42nd so as to be near his son, when the line halted he continued to walk forward coolly and deliberately until within a few steps of the enemy's lines and seeing that he was alone turned to walk back but had gone but a few steps before he fell dead near where his son had been killed but a few minutes before. When our line halted Pres. Gilder, the color bearer of the 40th Ala., was standing with the colors pressed to his breast, when a ball pierced his heart, and in falling he covered the flag he loved so well, and had carried so gallantly, with his heart's blood. Just as we were being withdrawn Maney's Brigade came in on our right and made a fierce assault, but all of no avail.

The loss not only in Baker's Brigade but in the whole of Stewart's Division was fearful, and all a useless sacrifice as Gen. Johnston had countermanded the order for the attack, but Gen. Hood had failed to communicate the same to Gen. Stewart.[30]

Our Southern Home September 14, 1899

Our dead and many of our wounded were left on the field in front of the enemy's lines. Mr. William Buntin of the 42nd Ala. who lived near Vienna in Pickens County fell, shot through the loins and was reported among the killed. Months passed and his wife who heard nothing further from him put on mourning, counting him as dead. In June or July 1865 after most of the soldiers had returned home, she saw two gentlemen ride up and stop in front of the gate in a buggy, one of them got out and walked into the yard within a few steps of her before she recognized him. He lived many years one of the best and most useful citizens of Pickens County. He gave me a full account of his capture and imprisonment together with his suffering from cold and hunger. Many of the incidents of war, sound almost as strange as fiction.

After our repulse the division fell back to a ridge in our rear somewhat in advance of our former position. Soon after we had formed our line Col. Higley paid Lieut. Joe Knighton of Co. F and myself the compliment of selecting our companies—A and F—to occupy the post of danger in supporting a battery in an advanced position as it was supposed that the enemy would advance, and their main effort would be directed against this battery. But they were evidently satisfied to hold what they had, and did not advance outside their works.

The Rev. Mr. McMullen had been in the habit of having evening prayers with each regiment in our brigade and not making his appearance, Col. Higley came to me and requested me to go down the line to where the 42nd was and ask him to come up. I found Col. Lanier sitting at the root of a tree looking very sad and dejected. I delivered Col. Higley's message when Col. Lanier replied "Mr. McMullen is dead sir." Gen. Stewart who was riding by heard his reply, and turning to me, said "What is that?" I told him that Col. Lanier had just told me that Mr. McMullen had been killed. He seemed overcome for a few moments saying, "Oh what a pity! What a pity! Why did he go in there!"

The enemy having crossed the river some distance below Resaca, with a large force endangering our rear, our army fell back, the movement beginning about midnight. Stewart's Division covered the rear crossing the river just before daylight. As we were crossing the pontoon bridge just above the railroad bridge, that structure was a mass of flames, and the enemy knowing from this that we were falling back, began shelling vigorously, but fortunately they did not have our range. After crossing the river we had a few hours much needed rest, and then resumed our march in the direction of Calhoun.

Adairsville

[continued from Our Southern Home September 14, 1899]

Near Adairsville we met the advance of the enemy and a lively fight ensued for some time. Our division was not engaged, being held in reserve. About this time it commenced raining and heavy showers fell every day for about forty or fifty days. The roads were badly cut up by wagons, artillery and horses, and the men were forced to march through mud and water and lie down at night on the wet ground in their wet clothes. In addition to this we carried three day's rations consisting of corn bread and bacon. The bread was cooked in thick pones, and after the second day would be so filled with mould that when it was broken it looked like it was filled with spider webs. When we had an opportunity to do so, we would make a little fire and toast the bread and broil the meat. During this campaign the men were ravenous for vegetable diet, but even if they could have gotten the vegetables they had no way of cooking them. Upon one occasion some of the men in our regiment got a camp kettle and I saw them gathering potato tops, poke salad, lambsquarter and even the careless weed which they cooked and ate with a relish.

The enemy still manoeuvering to turn our flank and get into our rear, we were constantly changing position to meet each of their movements, and all this time the rattle of musketry and booming of artillery

96

was kept up without cessation, day and night. Never did two gladiators in the arena watch each other more closely than Johnston and Sherman watched each other. About this time our forces all told amounted to about sixty-three thousand men, while that of the enemy amounted to about one hundred and ten thousand.[31]

From Adairsville we moved to Kingston and from Kingston to Cassville where line of battle was formed and the battle order read to each regiment. Of course we expected a big battle, but after skirmishing throughout the day we fell back during the night. It seems that after Gen. Johnston had issued his battle order, that Gens. Hood and Polk stated that their positions were such that they could not hold them and insisted upon falling back while Gen. Hardee expressed himself as being confident of his ability to hold his part of the line. The men were very much disappointed as they wanted to have one big battle and have the matter decided one way or the other. After retiring from Cassville we moved in the direction of Cartersville.[32]

Hood's Corps had been shifted in the different movements that took place from the extreme left of our army. After remaining in this position several days, constantly fighting, marching and counter-marching, another change was made which brought Hood's Corps in position on the right not far from New Hope Church. We took our position on the morning of the 25th, Stewart's division in front and facing west, but about one o'clock our position was changed to face nearly north, to meet the enemy coming from that direction. In this position we fought the battle of New Hope Church, which will form the subject of my next article.

Battle of New Hope Church

Our Southern Home November 2, 1899

On May the 25th, about noon Stewart's Division reached New

Hope Church. The spring rains had set in a week or ten days before rendering the roads almost impassable for artillery, and wagons, and interfering with the rapid movement of troops. The remainder of Hood's Corps was somewhere in the rear, and we had halted near New Hope Church—an old log house—had stacked arms, and were engaged in broiling bacon and toasting corn bread, in order to dry out the "cob webs" as some of the boys called the mould formed in it, when away off to the right, and north of us was heard an occasional shot, and then more frequently until it developed into an almost continuous roar. Soon you could hear the command from all directions, "fall in," and in a few minutes Stewart's Division was in line ready to meet the enemy. Clayton's Brigade was on the left, Stovall's on the right with Baker's in the center, while our artillery was planted on the New Hope Church Road and to the left of Baker's Brigade. The skirmish line in our front consisted of the 32nd and 58th Alabama and Austin's sharp shooters, commanded by Col. Bush Jones. As an evidence of the stubborn resistance offered to the enemy, I will state that although contending against Hooker's entire corps, it took the enemy something like two hours to drive this little force about one mile. Col. Jones had orders to hold his ground just as long as it was possible to do so, as it was important to gain as much time as we could in order that the other divisions of our corps might come up. But after all, Stewart alone and single handed had to meet the attack of the entire 20th corps of the Federal army, under the command of Gen. Hooker, a fine body of troops and a fighting general to lead them. I had made it a point to see that my company was provided with axes, and always had two if I had to carry one myself. When the firing in front indicated that we were about to be attacked. I had three trees, each about a foot in diameter, cut down the limbs trimmed off, and with them constructed a little breast work that proved very valuable, for while the companies on my right and left suffered severely, I did not have a man hurt during the first evening of the battle.[33]

About the center of my company was a hickory tree a little larger than my body and I took my position behind this, standing up so that I could have a full survey of the whole field. Our position was on the edge of a little branch, in our front was a long stretch of slightly undulating ground, and in our rear a slight elevation running parallel to the little stream in our front. The ground upon which the battle was fought was in the woods, but there was but little undergrowth, so in my position I had a fine view. Our skirmishers had not been in long before great masses of the enemy in four or five lines appeared in our front. They came on in splendid style with flags waving and their guns shining in the bright sunlight—the sun making its appearance after one of the heavy showers we had been having for several days, and by the way which continued for the proverbial "forty days and forty nights." Our artillery—sixteen pieces were massed at one point—opened upon the enemy, but they continued to advance until within range of our small arms when a blaze shot from our line, and was promptly responded to by the enemy.[34] But our fire was more than they could stand and they fell back to the tune of shells, minnie balls and rebel yells. No sooner had this line disappeared than we heard the huzza, huzza, huzza of the Federals—this being their way of cheering—and we knew that we would have but a brief breathing spell. Sure enough in a few minutes another magnificent line advanced and reached the same point reached by the first line when they were met by the same withering fire which their friends had met a few minutes before, and like the first line, they too gave way followed by our yells. But our yells had scarcely died away before their loud huzzas warned us that another charge was about to be made, and sure enough, before the smoke from the other charges had lifted, another long line of blue was seen emerging from the woods in the distance and on they came, reaching a point still nearer our line and making a more determined effort than either of the others. I noticed a color bearer with a magnificent flag, when the line halted, plant his flag and gathering its folds press it to his breast. In a few moments he was enveloped in smoke, and when the charge was over and the smoke drifted away I could see neither flag nor bearer. It is to be hoped that he escaped safely with the object of his affection still pressed to his breast. Thus two hours or more the battle raged; charge after charge, advancing with cheers, like waves beating against the rock bound coast, they were thrown back shattered, followed by loud yells and cheers of triumph. One single division in a single line had met and repulsed every attack of one of the best corps of the Federal army.[35]

No wonder Gen. Stewart was proud of his division. After the battle for the evening was over he rode down the line, tears streaming down his face as much for joy at the victory as for sorrow, for his dead and dying soldiers, that strewed the way. During the fight Gibson's Louisiana brigade arrived in our rear, and one of his regiments—the 16th Louisiana I think—performed as pretty an evolution as I ever saw on the battlefield. Thinking doubtless, that we were hard pressed and needed assistance they came on in column at double quick until the head of the column reached the little ridge that I have spoken of, in rear of our position, when the order was given, "Change front forward on first company," and right there under fire the movement was executed like clockwork. It was a fine but unnecessary display of discipline. Finding that they were not needed, they retired in a few minutes behind the crest of the little ridge on which they had so splendidly formed.

Home Sweet Home

[continued from Our Southern Home November 2, 1899]

The battle was over, the smoke had lifted; the western heavens were lit up by the golden light of a beautiful sun set; the young leaves had put forth and pendant to each was a rain drop sparkling and glistening in the sunshine like beautiful gems. It was a beautiful May day evening, balmy and sweet, well calculated to fill the heart with love and thoughts of home. All at once a Federal band, distant not more than six or eight hundred yards, began to play and played beautifully "Star Spangled Banner," and when it ceased the Federal soldiers cheered and huzzaed. A moment later, and very much to our surprise the band of the Louisiana regiment just in our rear, struck up "Dixie" and played it splendidly, and when it ceased playing, we yelled and cheered, and yelled only as a lot of old Confederates could yell. As soon as we ceased the Federal band struck up "Yankee Doodle" and when it finished, they huzzaed and cheered again, and then our band struck up "The Bonnie Blue Flag" and we cheered and yelled again. Scarcely had our cheers ceased, before softly and sweetly came floating on the evening air from the Federal band "Home Sweet Home." They finished, but there was neither huzza, nor cheer, but all around could be seen stern men with their faces blackened with the smoke of battle, wiping away with their rough jacket sleeves, the tears that trickled down their faces. The sad duty of burying the dead having been performed we lay down on the wet ground to rest, knowing that tomorrow would bring a renewal of the struggle.

Our Southern Home November 9, 1899

During the night of the 25th the remainder of our corps, and Hardee's Corps came up, Polk's Corps bringing up the rear the next morning. The fight in our immediate front opened early on the morning of the 26th with a lively skirmish, but no general advance was made. It soon developed that the entire Federal army was in our front and were extending their left so as to overlap our right, but Hardee was there with his three veteran divisions to meet them. So the fighting, except on the skirmish line, shifted from our front to the right, where repeated efforts were made by the enemy to drive

Hardee from his position, but they failed to do so. The fighting on this day was not continuous, but spasmodic, shifting from point to point along the entire right wing of our army as if seeking some vulnerable point. Just after dark three companies from the 40th Ala., were detailed as skirmishers to cover Baker's Brigade. I, in command of Co. A, covered the 37th Ala. Capt. E. D. Willett in command of Co. B, covered the 40th Ala., and Capt. A. M. Moore, in command of Co. K, covered the 37th [sic, *42nd*] and 54th Ala.

While we moved out as quietly and cautiously as possible, we were nevertheless discovered and subjected to a severe fire which was kept up without intermission during the entire night. The fire on the skirmish line was kept up furiously all day, infantry and artillery joining in the fight; their line was increased in strength until it amounted to a line of battle. In passing up and down the line of my company, some hundred yards or more in length, I was shot at hundreds of times and never received a scratch. While standing near a little branch watching the effects of the enemy's shell that were passing through a tall popular at the root of which a group of my men were lying, a shell or large round shot fell in the water at my feet. If it was a shell, fortunately for me it did not explode, but at all events I was literally covered with water and mud and sand.

Too Rough a Litter Ride

[continued from Our Southern Home November 9, 1899]

Some very amusing things occurred in almost every battle, and one occurred here. The left wing of the company was under the command of Lieut. W. Y. Peteet, as brave and gallant a man as ever drew the breath of life. The custom was for the litter bearers to remain at a safe distance in the rear until some one was wounded and then they would be sent for or called to come and carry the wounded man off, if he was unable to walk. The litter was a stretcher—a piece of strong canvas tacked to two poles—and generally required four men to handle it. About the middle of the afternoon away up the line where Lieut. Peteet was, I heard some one cry out and I knew that one of my men had been wounded. I immediately called to Peteet to know who it was and he answered that it was Yarborough. I asked if he was able to get out without assistance and he replied that Yarborough said he was not. I thereupon sent to the rear for the litter bearers, and they not knowing where the wounded man was came directly to me at the center of the line, and when they reached me I sent them up the line to where he lay. There were four of them and all this time they were exposed to the enemy's fire. They proceeded up the line and placed Yarborough, who weighed about one hundred and seventy-five pounds, on the litter, and instead of going back in a straight line to the rear they came back the same way they went in. As they approached me I noticed they were stooping very low and dragging Yarborough along so close to the ground that his back was getting the benefit of every root, rock or pine knot on the way, and just as they got opposite to where I was standing, Yarborough thinking that the mode of travel was a little rough, and not as fast as it ought to be, jumped off the litter, and the last I saw of them Yarborough was leading in a bee line for the rear with the litter bearers in the wake cursing him for all they were worth for so unnecessarily exposing them. Yarborough had been shot through the shoulder, and what that had to do with his legs was something more than the litter bearers could understand.

Shortly before sundown a large reinforcement was added to the line in our front, which could be seen advancing and deploying, and a fresh battery was opened, not more than two hundred and fifty yards. Under these circumstances we were ordered to fall back to our lines, consequently we fell back to the 37th Ala.

The 37th was protected by a frail line of breast works of rails and dirt, through which the shot and shell of the enemy passed as if it had been so much straw. After we got within the lines of the 37th and while I was sitting by the side of Capt. Greene, of that regiment, a minnie ball striking the limb of a tree, glanced striking him on the nose, skinning it as it went and striking me on the right arm just above the elbow; in a few minutes another struck me on the right thigh, neither doing any damage.

Premature Burial

[continued from Our Southern Home November 9, 1899]

When my men came in, having been up two nights, with nothing to eat, exhausted from loss of sleep and hunger, they threw themselves down on the ground, and in a few minutes were fast asleep. After resting a short time I proceeded down the line to report to Col. Higley for orders, and when I returned about dark, I was informed that Sergeant William S. Allison who had been by my side all day, had been killed by a minnie ball in the head, and that N. B. Dearman and R. J. McGowen together with five or six others of the 37th Ala. had been killed by the explosion of a shell, as they lay asleep upon the ground where they had lain down when we came in. Several others had been wounded but none seriously. I ordered the dead buried and was very much surprised next morning to see McGowen walking around.

It seems that when the burying squad went to perform their duties, they came to McGowen last, and as they took him up to roll him in his blanket preparatory to laying him in the grave, he gave a kick, and he was laid down and in a few minutes was able to sit up, having been stunned and rendered unconscious by the concussion and shock of the shell that had sent death and destruction to so many of his comrades. He lived to pass through the remainder of the war and died only a few years ago. A few minutes more to the horrors of war, would have been added that of being buried alive.

That night our corps was relieved by Polk's Corps and we were marched back to the rear, where we could rest after three days and nights of almost continuous fighting. While we were thus engaged on the left, the enemy had moved to our right, and thinking they could overwhelm that part of our line as they had attempted to do on the left, they made a furious attack, but they found a lion in their pathway in the person of Cleburne and his division. The fighting was fast and furious, and although Cleburne was overlapped and flanked, he faced one of his brigades to the rear, and meeting the enemy front and rear drove them off with fearful slaughter. The 107th New York was practically destroyed, losing perhaps the largest percentage of any regiment in the Federal army during the war. The enemy had good reason to remember the battle of Pumpkin Vine Creek, as they called it, for their loss amounted to five to six thousand, killed and wounded.[36] A gentleman who visited the field of battle, in the fall of 1864 told me that he counted seven hundred Federal graves at and near New Hope Church. This is a wonderful loss when we consider that on the Confederate side, but two divisions—Stewart's and Cleburne's participated to any considerable extent in the fight. During the entire time we were engaged around New Hope Church the men were drenched with rain; almost every hour of the day there was a down pour of rain and before we could get dry, there would be another. I don't suppose there is an old soldier of the Army of Tennessee who will forget as long as he lives, the experience of those days. It taxes the credulity of the present generation to believe that men could endure what we did and live.

Our Southern Home November 16, 1899

In my article of the 3rd, in speaking of the skirmish line in our front commanded by Col. Bush Jones, I spoke of the 58th Ala. as being on the skirmish line when it should have been the 54th Ala. I make this correction at the suggestion of my friend P.E. Ward, who was a member of the 55th [sic, *54th*]Ala., and was present and participated in the fighting around New Hope Church. And right here I would like to say to all old army friends, that as I am writing from memory, and thirty-five years is a good long period, I would be glad, when I fall into error, to have my attention called to it, as that I can correct it.

Brothers Die

[*continued from* Our Southern Home *November 16, 1899]*

After our corps had been relieved by Polk's Corps, we had a day's rest in the rear, where stray bullets and shells were constantly falling. Among others my brother James, who belonged to the 42nd Ala. was mortally wounded. I was with him in a short time after he was carried to the field hospital in our rear, and told him the surgeon said that he was mortally wounded and could live but a short time. He simply remarked, "I would like to live for the sake of my wife and children. I have tried to do my duty." Of such were the heroes of the Confederate army. Every hour in the day witnessed such pathetic scenes—there was but little time for tears—a clasp of the hand—a loving look in the eyes—and on we went to other scenes of conflict and carnage. In the battle of New Hope Church Col. L. T. Woodruff of the 36th Ala., Clayton's Brigade, was dangerously wounded, but refused to leave the field—taking his seat at the foot of a tree he continued to command his regiment, exposed all the time to the fire of the enemy. A captain in the 37th Ala.—I have forgotten his name— while opening his mouth to give a command, was shot, the ball entering while his mouth was open and penetrating the back part of his mouth, coming out near the base of the skull in the rear, and yet in a few weeks he was back in command of his company.

Noonday Creek

[continued from <u>Our Southern Home</u> November 16, 1899]

The rains were almost continuous and that night we fell back or rather changed our position to the right to meet a movement of the enemy in that direction—it rained in torrents; the mud was axle deep to the wagons, artillery, caissons, and the ambulances. The teams moved by torch light and it frequently took an hour to move a mile. Of course our movements were slower as brigades and divisions had to wait for those in front of them to move and sometimes this necessitated standing in the mud and water for an hour at a time. Oh, the long weary hours we thus stood. It is almost beyond belief that human beings could endure what we endured. From here on the grand game of war was played between Sherman with one hundred and ten thousand men and Gen. Joe Johnston with sixty-four thousand and in all this grand strategy never did Joe Johnston make a mistake. He retreated no further than Lee did in Virginia, did not lose as many men or pieces of artillery, and inflicted a loss upon the enemy equal to his entire force, and yet after one of the most magnificent campaigns on record, and with the hearty support of every private, field officer and general of brigade, division and corps—save one—he was removed.

While the removal of Gen'l Johnston has nothing to do with the narrative, still as an old Confederate, we feel indignant at the treatment of our old commander. By an examination of the map of Georgia it will be seen that we were far down to the left from the line of railroad leading from Atlanta to Chattanooga. As Gen. Sherman ascertained that he could not pass our left as he had attempted at New Hope Church, he commenced shifting to our right as Grant did with

Lee after the battle of the Wilderness, and day by day, and night after night the changing, shifting and fighting went on without cessation, passing from the west to the east of the railroad to Ackworth, and from there to Shantie Town [Big Shanty], and from there to Burnt Station [Hickory], and from there to Noonday Creek, where we spent several days. An account of the action at this place and subsequent movement will be treated in the next article.

Our Southern Home November 30, 1899

I have another correction to make. In my last article I said or intended to say, that P.E. Ward belonged to the 54th Ala., and the types made me say 55th.

On the night of the 14th of June our regiment was sent to relieve a regiment belonging to some other command, on picket duty, nearly a mile in our front. The general direction of the line was east and west but a part of the line occupied by our regiment had been forced back a few days before and a new line formed so as to be almost north and south and facing west, necessarily forming an acute angle at the point where the new line connected with the line as originally formed.

On this new part of the line were companies A, C, and E. Company C under command of Capt. T. M. Brunson with Lieuts. J. W. Monette and N. E. Thomas was on the left, Co. A commanded by myself with Lieut. W. Y. Peteet, came next, Co. E commanded by Lieut. E. H. Ward was to my right and occupied the angle I have spoken of, being the most exposed position on the whole line. To the right of Lieut. Ward the other companies of the regiment except Co. B held in reserve, were formed, but in what order, I do not now remember. The following officers were in command:

Co. D commanded by Capt. A. G. Campbell with Lieuts. Williams and Vinson. Co. F commanded by Lieuts. J. H. Knighton and J.

Wesley Johnston. Co. G commanded by Lieuts. Collier and Going; Co. H by Lieuts. Hicks and Howell. Co. I commanded by Capt. Hiram Grant with Lieuts. Shater and Moore; and Co. K commanded by Capt. A. M. Moore with Lieuts. W. B. Bingham; and B. B. Sanders. Co. B in reserve was commanded by Capt. E. D. Willett; and Lieuts. J. A. Latham and Ed. Vance, and with this company was Col. Joe H. Higley, Adjutant Clarence H. Ellerbee and Sergeant Major W. P. Hall.

Lightning Strikes

[continued from Our Southern Home November 30, 1899]

I am thus particular in giving the names of all the officers on duty that day to correct a statement made by Gen. O. O. Howard of the Federal army in *Century Magazine* a few years ago. The rifle pits occupied by us were nothing but shallow holes in the ground with a few rails and a little dirt in front. Just behind us was a high rail fence and about two hundred yards in our rear was Noonday Creek, a good sized stream about waist deep. Our line was in an old field some two hundred yards from the edge of the woods occupied by the enemy. The morning of June the 15th, 1864, opened bright and clear and as the day advanced the heat from the vertical rays of a summer sun was scorching. The men were crowded in the rifle pits in a cramped position without shade or water, and exposed from daylight until the middle of the afternoon to an incessant fire of shot and shell. Away off to our right we could see troops being massed by the enemy, and in our immediate front we knew from the increased infantry and artillery fire that we were contending against a regular line of battle. During the morning we had been annoyed by the enemy's sharpshooters. It was dangerous for one to expose his head for a moment. John Anderson of Co. A was killed by being shot in the head and several others wounded. Mark Bolling had picked up on the battlefield of Chickamauga an Enfield rifle with a cylinder like a pistol; it was a five shooter. It had a hammer that was five or six inches long, and not being in the center like the hammer of a pistol, it had to be extra long and twisted to one side so as to strike the caps on the tubes of the cylinder. It certainly was a curiosity in the way of a firearm; the boys used to tell Mark that the hammer went to h—l for fire and brought back a chunk. Mark concluded that he would play a trick on the Yankee sharpshooter and draw his fire; he laid his gun on the top of the rifle-pit as near in the direction of the enemy as he could, and fired; in an instant came the zip of the enemy's bullet in answer, and Mark raised himself to take deliberate aim when zip came another and split the skin of his head from front to rear. Being bald on the top of his head it looked like a streak of lightning had struck him. He was badly stunned but finally pulled himself together, grabbed his fuses and started for the rear with the Yankees shooting at him every jump, but he made it through all right. About two o'clock it became evident that our little skirmish line would be attacked by an overwhelming force. They could see very plainly that our line of battle was a mile in the rear and that we were without support—not a single piece of artillery being so placed as to give us any assistance. I called to Lieut. Ward, who as I have said occupied the most exposed position on the line, and told him that I would hold my position as long as he held his in order for him to get out if it became necessary to fall back. The firing was getting heavier every minute, new batteries were being opened and the enemy was pressing up from every direction. I looked away across the old field, to our line a mile away, and my heart sank as I thought of traversing that distance exposed to shot and shell—a high fence and creek waist deep in our rear, with no protection—nothing but a bare open field, not even a sapling to protect us from this concentrated fire.

Retreat

[continued from <u>Our Southern Home</u> November 30, 1899]

Agony and suspense must have an end, and finally ours was ended. About three o'clock looking across to my right on the other side of Noonday Creek nearly a mile away I saw our line was broken—point after point being carried. I had but little time however to watch these movements, for about that time the advance was made in force on our part of the line. Almost before I could realize what was taking place the enemy were in the little redoubt held by Lieut. Ward. Seeing that prompt action was necessary I ordered the men to fire and then take care of themselves. They arose, delivered a volley into the ranks of the enemy, not more than thirty or forty yards away, and then started across the old field in our rear.

It is useless to describe the scene that followed, it was simply a race for liberty at the risk of life or limb. I was determined not to be captured, although a big Yankee was very close to me crying halt at every step, and shooting at me as fast as he could. I thought he could load and shoot faster than any fellow I ever saw. Finally I got to the bank of the creek; he shot at me again and missed me and when I waddled up the bank on the other side the rascal was loading as fast as he could, and as I was too heavy to run he had ample time to load and shoot again which he did, taking deliberate aim, and missed me. After crossing the creek and going a short distance we were exposed to the concentrated fire of the Federal batteries, the infantry stopping at the creek. We had quite a number of men killed and wounded and among others Tom Green of Co. A was mortally wounded. In a former article I stated that he was killed at the battle of Bentonville, but this was a mistake.

Howard Refuted

[continued from Our Southern Home November 30, 1899]

Now for the statement of Gen. O. O. Howard, as published in the *Century Magazine*. In his article he stated that upon this occasion he captured the entire 40th Ala. On the contrary he captured only a small part of it. He did not capture the colonel, lieut. colonel, major, adjutant, sergeant major, or the flag. Of the company officers he captured none of Co. A and only seven or eight men, and among them Sergeant Lowry, Lewis Lancaster, Jas. Pullian, W. C. Lewis and perhaps one or two others whose names I cannot now recall. Of Co. B which was in reserve, not an officer or man was captured. Co. C lost no officer and but a few men. Co. G lost two officers, Lieuts. Collier and Going and a part of the company. Co. H two officers, Lieuts. Hicks and Howell and over half of the men; Co. I lost three officers, Capt. Gantt and Lieuts. Shafer and Moore and over half of the company, Co. K lost three officers, Capt. A. M. Moore and Lieuts. Bingham and Sanders with nearly the entire company.

I suppose if Gen. Howard captured the entire regiment he furnished the war department with a list of officers, field and staff, and also company officers, and can tell what became of the flag, etc. For his information we will say that the 40th Alabama surrendered at Salisbury, N.C., and that the flag that floated over us on the 15th day of June, 1864 is now in Livingston, and never was captured or surrendered. And among the names of the officers given above not more than one-third were captured, and about the same proportion of the men. Such is history.

For some unexplained reason Gen. Hood never possessed the confidence of his corps. His bravery and devotion to the cause of the Confederacy no one ever doubted; of both he had given too many evidences on hard fought fields to question either. His presence never aroused any enthusiasm. It may be that the soldiers resented the promotion and transfer of a major general from the Army of Northern Virginia, when such men as Pat Cleburne, W. H. T. Walker, A. P. Stewart, John C. Breckenridge and others, who had long commanded divisions in the Army of Tennessee, and who were known and loved by their men, were available. There is an explanation to this, however, which it is useless to discuss at this time. Suffice it is to say the soldiers of Hood's Corps felt that he might be a splendid brigade commander, or fairly good division commander, but that as a corps commander he was a failure. The disaster of the 15th of June at Noonday Creek following the terrific slaughter of Stewart's Division at Resaca in attacking the enemy behind breast works, confirmed this opinion. Like some of Napoleon's marshals he was a hard fighter when guided and directed by a master mind, but when left largely to his own resources, like them, failed.

Kennesaw Mountain

[continued from Our Southern Home December 14, 1899]

On the 16th of June, we were moved to the right, and on the 17th, were in position near Kennesaw Mountain, where our division had a rest for a day in a valley to the South. This was the first day's rest we had had since the campaign opened, and the men utilized it to change clothing and wash off some of the mud and dirt that had accumulated on their persons. The rains of which I have spoken in a previous article had continued to pour down in torrents, and this was the first day that passed without a down pour of rain.

A Rattler

[contined from Our Southern Home December 14, 1899]

We had been living during the entire campaign on toasted cornbread, and broiled bacon, and the men were nearly crazy for vegetable diet. Some few men had camp kettles and they determined to have salad for dinner. I saw men gathering poke salad, potato tops, lamb's quarters, and even the tender shoots of the careless weed, and put all in the same pot and boil until thoroughly cooked, and then eat with a relish. That night about 12 o'clock we were ordered to ascend Kennesaw Mountain to support French's Division which was holding the crest of the mountain. We passed up the side of the mountain, which was steep and rugged in line of battle. As we went up I heard a peculiar sound—once heard never forgotten—that of a rattlesnake. Strange to say the line had passed over it, and not a man had been bitten. I being in rear of my company doubtless would have been, but for his snakeship's timely warning. Drawing my sword I hacked and whacked away in the direction from which the sound issued, and presently I heard a dull heavy thud of a lick, and the blood curdling sound died away, and I knew that I had dealt a mortal blow. We halted on the plateau, just behind the crest of a mountain on which a battery was placed. I would remark here that I slept that night, or rather the remainder of it, on the biggest, broadest, highest rock I could find. I didn't want any rattlesnakes for bed-fellows.

A Visit to Ector's Brigade

[continued from Our Southern Home December 14, 1899]

The next day having nothing else to do, and the shells falling and exploding about as thick in one place as another and it being about as safe on the top of the mountain where the line of battle was located, as where we were, I concluded that I would go up and take a survey of the field. It was indeed a grand view. For miles around, in a great semi-circle could be seen the lines of the Federal army and every hundred yards or so a battery from which issued puffs of smoke and then screaming and tearing through the air came shells, exploding like claps of thunder, scattering their fragments, and whistling and singing in all directions. Our batteries were replying, and we could see the shells from our guns drop right into their batteries and line of battle. I soon ascertained that we were supporting our old friends, Ector's Texas brigade. I found Gen. Ector under a tentfly just back of his line. He was delighted to see me and gave me a cordial invitation to stay and take dinner with him. I can't say that "n'ere consenting I consented" for seeing a pan full of nice biscuits and a pot of good strong coffee I promptly accepted the invitation, and I think I cleaned the platter.

While the General and I were eating dinner his little son, not more than fourteen or fifteen years old, came bounding down from the battery, around which shells were exploding thick and fast, with face all aglow and eyes sparkling and said, "Papa, I tell you our battery is tearing them Yankees all to pieces." I have written of the father. What became of the son I know not, but if the heroism of the sire descends to the son, and he still lives, there is a grand and noble character to impress itself upon his fellowmen.

The fight around the whole line was incessant; not a moment, day or night that there was not the booming of cannon or the crack of small arms, with an occasional charge from the enemy on some part of our line, which in every instance was repulsed with severe loss to them.

While on this line a terrific assault was made by the enemy on Hardee's Corps, falling principally on Cheatham's and Cleburne's divisions. The charge was so determined that the enemy approached so near our lines that when the attack failed quite a number of them were captured and among them a little Irishman who inquired what command it was into whose hands he had fallen, and being told that it was Cleburne's Division, said, "It is Cleburne on the right, Cleburne on the left and I'll be d—d if don't believe its Cleburne all around." Pat was proud of his fellow countryman even if he was opposed to him. The Federal loss in this attack was very heavy while ours was comparatively small, being well protected.

Kolb's Farm

Our Southern Home December 28, 1899

We remained in position on the line around Kennesaw Mountain for a week or more. The fighting was incessant—the troops being shifted from one position to another to meet the movements of the enemy. About the 20th or 21st, a considerable force of the enemy crossed a creek the name of which I have now forgotten, somewhat to our left, occupying a position somewhat isolated from the main body of the enemy. The creek at that point made a considerable bend, and the line of the enemy was across the neck of the bend. Inasmuch as this portion of the enemy's force seemed to be detached from the main body, Gen. Hood conceived the idea of attacking and crushing them in their position, and for that purpose moved our corps in that direction with Stevenson's and Hindman's divisions in front, ours (Stewart's) in reserve. It was the first time that I can recall during

116

the campaign where Stewart's Division was held in reserve. And I will here remark that it is no pleasant thing to be held in reserve. Every old soldier will tell you that of all the trying ordeals the most trying is to stand, perhaps for an hour, with the battle raging in front, expecting every moment to hear the order "Forward!"

In this case the battle was raging furiously, and there we stood the stragglers and wounded streaming to the rear. One poor fellow came hobbling along scarcely able to walk and said "Go in there boys and you will catch h-ll." Fortunately for us we were not ordered in, Stevenson's and Hindman's divisions had met a bloody repulse, losing a thousand men in less than one hour. Instead of the enemy being isolated and unprotected it turned out that after crossing the creek they had thrown up strong breast works across the narrow neck, while their flanks were protected by the creek, and it was against this strongly fortified position, well defended by both infantry and artillery that Gen. Hood hurled his corps.[37] We held the line around Kennesaw until about the first or second of July, when the movements of the enemy to our left caused us to move so as to meet the movements of the enemy. The disparity of numbers was so great at this time that it was an easy matter for the enemy to throw a force of one-half of our entire army to right or left, and thus force us out of position that would otherwise have been impregnable. In this way our army was forced from its position around Kennesaw and Marietta.

Retreat to the Chattahoochee River

[continued from Our Southern Home December 28, 1899]

On the morning of July 6th, after marching all night, we took our position on the main road to Atlanta, across the Chattahoochee River. A pretty good line of entrenchments had been erected, and we supposed that we would have several days rest, but that night the 40th

Alabama was ordered on picket, and this meant twenty-four hours on duty. The next day while with my company on picket, it being necessarily hot, I was trying to take things easy lying flat on my back gazing up at a jay bird complacently picking himself on the limb of a large white oak tree under which I was lying when very unexpectedly to myself and also to Mr. Jay Bird a Federal battery opened, and boom-burer-er twisting and tearing through the branches of the tree came a shell not far from where the jay bird sat. He seemed to be paralyzed for a moment, but only for a moment, when he bounded about ten feet in the air, crying jay, jay, and struck a bee-line in the direction of Atlanta, crying jay-jay at every flap of his wings. I felt at the time as if I would like to be a jay bird myself.

Fifteen-Year-Old Cadets

[continued from Our Southern Home December 28, 1899]

This reminds me of the joke that was told on one of the South Carolina cadets at the battle of Kingston in North Carolina about the first of March, 1865. Some of the little fellows were not more than fifteen years old, and while most of this gallant band of little fellows stood the fire like veterans, one of them became demoralized and was making his way to the rear as fast as his little legs could carry him, with the tears streaming down his face as he thought of home and mother when a staff officer met him, and sternly commanded him to halt, saying "Ain't you ashamed to be running away and crying like a baby." The little fellow between his sobs managed to say, "Y-e-e-s, I wish I was a baby, and a gal baby at that." He wanted to put it beyond all peradventure that he would never be caught in another war.

The last I saw of this gallant little corps they were at Raleigh, N.C., on their way home, and they bore themselves like veterans;

they were boy heroes. What would the mothers of today think of sending to the battle front their fifteen year old boys! Oh, the fervid patriotism and devotion of the women of the South during that long, fearful struggle—no artist can paint nor pen portray.

Joe Johnston Relieved of Command

Our Southern Home January 25, 1900

On the 18th of July, 1864, General Joseph E. Johnston was relieved of the command of the Army of Tennessee, and Gen. John B. Hood, who had been advanced to the full grade of general, was placed in command.

No calamity, could have befallen the Southern Confederacy equal to this, unless it had been to remove Gen. Lee from the command of the Army of Virginia, and place General Early or some other Lieut. General in command of that army. General Johnston had accomplished everything that it was in the power of any general to accomplish with the forces at his command. He possessed the love and confidence of his men, and of all his generals save one or two. Such men as Hardee, Polk, Stewart, Cleburne, Cheatham, Walker, Hindman and others were devoted to him and in addition to this he had the unbounded confidence of Gen. R. E. Lee—the grandest character who figured in this grand drama. Surely there was merit in a man who was so esteemed. Nor is this all. The enemy recognized his ability. Gen. Sherman, when he heard of Gen. Johnston's removal, the day after it occurred, remarked to the officers who were with him, that the removal of Gen. Johnston was worth a reinforcement of 10,000 men to his army.

But it was said that the army was demoralized by the retrograde movements from Dalton to Atlanta. It was no more demoralized than the Army of Virginia was by its retrograde movement, caused by the same flanking processes by reason of superior numbers, from the Rapidan to Petersburg, and covering a greater distance than from Dalton to Atlanta. Again this is refuted by the desperate fighting

119

done by the Army of Tennessee on the 20th, 22nd and 28th of July, just a few days after Gen. Johnston was removed from the command of the army. From my own personal knowledge the morale of the army was better, and the men more confident than the day the campaign opened. As I have stated the officers and men had the most unbounded love for, and confidence in General Johnston. So great was it that had one regiment or brigade stacked arms, and refused to fight under Gen. Hood, almost the entire army would have done likewise. Some have censured President Davis very severely for removing General Johnston, attributing it to personal dislike. While I think it was a mistake, and exceedingly unfortunate that it should have been done, at the same time President Davis was too much of a patriot, and too much devoted to the cause of the South to allow his personal feelings to influence him in so important a matter. He was not infallible by any means, but in this case I think Gov. Brown, of Georgia, and Gen. Bragg more to blame than any one else.

On the 20th Stewart's Corps was heavily engaged attacking the enemy behind breast works, sustaining heavy loss, Gen. Stewart being severely wounded.[38] On the 21st, another attack was ordered, our corps, now commanded by Gen. Cheatham, since Gen. Hood's promotion, was to make the attack, supported by Hardee's Corps, but just about the time the movement was to begin, the order was countermanded. The point at which the attack was to be made was strongly fortified with all sorts of obstructions in front. The morning of the 22nd of July, Hardee's Corps being on our right moved round the left flank of the enemy, and caught Blair's Corps "in the air" and proceeded to double it up, driving all before them, capturing some 2,000 prisoners, and ten pieces of artillery. They were only saved by the timely arrival of Gen. McPherson, who was killed while trying to stem the tide of Hardee's success. Our loss was heavy, including Gen. W. H. T. Walker, of Georgia. The fighting all along the line continued day and night without intermission, the firing increasing at times in volume until it assumed the proportions of a battle.[39]

120

Battle of Peachtree Creek[40]

[continued from Our Southern Home January 25, 1900]

On the 28th was fought the bloody battle of Peachtree Creek [sic, *Ezra Church*]. Our corps now commanded by Gen. Stephen D. Lee, supported by Stewart's Corps, attacked the left wing of the enemy strongly entrenched. A part of Baker's Brigade got within a few yards of the enemy's breast works. Col. Green of the 37th Ala. was killed within twenty or thirty steps of their line. Gibson's Louisiana brigade preceded ours, and the ground was literally covered with their dead and wounded. The fighting was desperate, but useless. The enemy not only out-numbered us nearly two to one, but in addition to this were well protected.

The loss of the 40th Ala. in these battles was heavy. Lieut. Vance of Co. B was killed and Lieut. Baker of Co. G was wounded—losing a leg. Among the killed of Co. As I can now only recall Hiram Fincher and William Watkins and among the wounded Jake Kinsey and Wm. Brooks. There were others but their names have escaped me. Companies C and K from Sumter also lost heavily in killed and wounded.

The attack had been made and failed and our forces were withdrawn to their original position, where day after day the same old routine was kept up of fighting along the whole line night and day. All around for miles in a semicircle could be seen clouds of smoke arising from batteries and small arms, and the men lay down at night to sleep with the din and roar in their ears and awoke in the morning to hear the same music. About the 5th or 6th of August the picket from Baker's Brigade under command of Lieut. Col. Gulley moved out just after dark to relieve the pickets in our front. This was always dangerous either going in or coming out. In passing around a little hill Col. Gulley slipped and fell, his knee striking a sharp rock, which disabled him and he had to be sent to the rear. Being the senior officer present I had to take command. I relieved the pickets on duty and then took my place about the center of the line. About midnight a staff officer came to me and told me that I would be relieved about daylight, and when relieved to take my men and follow the brigade to Atlanta. At the appointed time we were relieved and proceeded to Atlanta as directed where we arrived a little after sunrise and found the entire brigade getting aboard a train, and in a few minutes we were in motion in the direction of Macon, Georgia. We were soon out of hearing of the thunder and roar of guns to which we had been listening for ninety days without cessation.

Removed to Mobile Bay

Our Southern Home February 1, 1900

When our brigade left Atlanta we supposed that we were being hurried off to meet a raid of Federal cavalry sent out to cut some of the railroad, in the rear of our army. Even this was a relief if only for a few days, to be exempt from the arduous duties required of us in front of the enemy. But when we reached Macon, Ga., Gen. Baker informed us that Mobile, Ala., was our destination. Forts Morgan and Gaines had fallen, and the Federal fleet had entered Mobile Bay, and it was supposed that a land force would be sent up to co-operate with the fleet, by opening the Tensaw River, and thus get above Mobile thereby rendering the batteries and obstructions across the bay held by us, useless. The Governor of Alabama, to meet this anticipated movement, had asked that an Alabama brigade be sent to that point, and Baker's Brigade was selected. There never was a happier, jollier lot of fellows. A lot of school boys turned out for a holiday would not have been happier or jollier. The trials, hardships and dangers of the campaign through which they had just passed were all forgotten, and on all sides could be heard songs, laughter and cheers. It took us about three days to make the trip to Hall's Landing, the terminus at that time of the Mobile and Montgomery R. R. On our way down after we had passed Pollard some five or six miles, W. D. Bustian, of Co. A, who was standing on top of a box car, was knocked off in passing over a bridge and falling between the cars, was run over and both his legs terribly mangled. The boys were making so much noise, together with the noise of the train, made it impossible to make the engineer hear the order to stop, and we ran several miles before we could make him understand that a man had been knocked off. He finally stopped at a small station and finding a locomotive there, I took the assistant surgeon and two or three men and started back to the place where he had been knocked off. When we got to the creek, a wide, shallow stream, we could see nothing of him. A man up the road a hundred yards or so, at a little flag station, called to us to come up there. When we got there we found Bustian lying on the platform. After he had been knocked off and fallen into the creek, he managed in his mangled condition to crawl to the edge of the water, and his groans attracted the attention of some persons walking up the railroad track, and they had gotten him out, and carried him up to the little platform, where we found him. We took him to Pollard where he died that night, and was buried the next day.

It was sad to reflect that one so stout and vigorous, after passing through all the dangers of battles and exposures likely to produce death, should meet death in such a manner. When we reached Hall's Landing, the command was about ready to move. We marched down the Tensaw to Blakely, and the next day moved on to Spanish Fort, which was being strongly fortified.

The next day I was ordered to take Co. A and relieve the cavalry pickets along the beach from the mouth of Dolive's [De Olive's] Creek to Montrose, making The Village head-quarters, being about the center of the line. We arrived at The Village about the middle of the afternoon and soon the whole of Co. A was in the bay bathing—"washing off the Georgia clay" as the boys said. It was the first time in three months that they had had the chance to bathe, and they enjoyed it to "the full." The Village was a small collection of houses, built by citizens of Mobile for the use of their families during the summer, but now unoccupied except two or three families who had remained. The scuppernong grape flourishes in that section, and the vines were loaded with the most delicious grapes. We were enable to get some vegetables, milk, butter, chickens, and fish without number, and no set of men ever did more ample justice to these various delicacies than we did. What a contrast to broiled bacon and mouldy cornbread.

Lieut. Peteet and myself walked down the beach about a mile, and found some cavalrymen seining. The seine must have been one hundred and fifty feet long, and just as we got there they were making a haul. Such quantities of fish I never before saw; they were piled upon the beach by the barrel full. I noticed the men picking out from the piles lying around certain fish and leaving others. I didn't understand it at the time, but found out in the course of time why they did it. They had told us to help ourselves, and borrowing a basket from an old gentleman who lived nearby, we filled it full, having at least a bushel and half or two bushels of fish. We lugged it back to camp a mile or more through the deep sand, getting to camp about sundown. We immediately put our negro servant to scaling and cleaning the fish for supper, and he continued to scale, clean and cook until midnight, and still we were hungry for fish. The fact is we had "packed" that load of fish that distance and then found out that we had "Hickory Shad," a fish composed of scales and bones. We now understood why the cavalrymen rejected them.

On the next day we relieved the cavalry and placed our pickets along the beach. Co. A at this time numbered about sixty men, which included portions of Companies I and K; their officers and a majority of the men of these companies having been captured on the 15th day of June at Noonday Creek, they had elected to come into our company. We had enough men to picket the entire line by going on duty every other day, but Lieut. Peteet and myself being the only officers present, were on duty every night. One of us would go on duty and remain until twelve o'clock, and then the other would go on for the remainder of the night and the next day, the one who had been on duty the latter part of the night before, would take the first part and so on. When relieved I would throw myself down on the sand and sleep until the hot rays of an August sun would awake me next morning.

General Dabney Maury was in command of the Department of the Gulf, with head-quarters in Mobile, and under him Gen. St. John Liddell of Louisiana, was in command of the division of the army on the eastern shore of Mobile Bay from near Ft. Morgan to Spanish Fort. His command consisted of Baker's Brigade, one or two Louisiana regiments, a regiment of state troops, and the 15th Confederate cavalry, numbering 1500 men, under command of Col. Harry Maury. The Federal fleet lay in the middle of the Bay in full view of our pickets, and every evening they would send out a vessel to do picket duty for the fleet. The *Metacomte* was the vessel that usually performed this duty, taking her station about a mile from the beach— near enough for us to read the name painted on the wheelhouse—she being an old side wheel vessel.

Our Southern Home February 8, 1900

The *Metacomte* generally left her station about daylight. One morning long after her usual time of leaving she was seen at the place where she had anchored the day before. It was soon discovered that she was aground; the tide had ebbed rapidly owing to a stiff breeze from the north, and before those aboard were aware of it she was resting on the sand. A messenger was immediately dispatched to Spanish Fort to notify Gen. Liddell with a request for artillery to attack her in her helpless condition. After a long delay a heavy siege piece drawn by oxen appeared, and we went to work to mount it. It was soon ascertained that the old piece was worthless. This being reported, a section of rifled field artillery was sent down that night. All this time the *Metacomte* was lying there helpless. As soon as it was light enough to see, the field piece opened, the first shot falling just astern and the second going just beyond the vessel.

In a few minutes we could see that she was moving, the tide having risen sufficiently for her to float. In a short time she was out of range, and we were sadly disappointed thinking that she was at our mercy. The monotony of picket duty was unbroken; day after day and week after week the same round of duty. We had fish in abundance. An old gentleman by the name of Yancey, who lived in The Village, and who understood the habits of the fish gave the boys the benefit of his experience. When the wind was from the south or southwest in the evening he would tell us that we could get plenty of flounders, shrimps and crabs the next morning, and sure enough the beach would be lined with them. The flounder is a very peculiar looking fish, resembling a large flat fish split open, and each half being a whole fish, with the eyes both on the same side. Mr. Yancey's explanation of the reason for these fish coming to the edge of the beach when the wind was from the south or southwest, was that it blew the salt water in from the gulf, which made them sick, and in order to avoid this, they came to the edge of the beach, where they lay with the nose just out of the water. We utilized the bayonets of our Enfield rifles in spearing the fish, fastening them on poles; the men soon became quite expert in sticking their bayonets through the fish then throwing them out on the beach.

While Co. A was on duty, I was in command of all that portion of our line south of Dolive's Creek, and citizen's living below the creek who wished to go to Mobile, or any point north of the creek, had to come to me to get a pass in order to enable them to pass the picket line near Spanish Fort. I had issued a great many passes, and my brother officers got off a good joke on me in connection therewith.

It seems that Gen. Liddell had given some one a pass to go to Mobile, and when he presented it to the picket at Dolive's Creek, he looked at it very carefully and then handed it back to him, and told him that it would not do; that he could not pass there unless his pass had the name of "that Lieut. Sprott at The Village on it." It was the only instance during the war, that I know of where the name of a 1st Lieut. was worth more than that of an acting major general.

Government by military force, even among those who are friendly to the cause represented by the soldiers, is harsh and arbitrary. I often think of an occurrence that took place while I was in command at The Village that goes to illustrate what I have just said. A citizen living nearby had lost a hog, and two boys living near him who were bad characters were suspected of having committed the larceny. Complaint having been made to me I immediately had them arrested and tried them. There being no evidence against them I discharged them, cautioning them to be very careful in future, as they might not get off so easy next time.

I was young and inexperienced and thought I was doing right, but I now know that it was an unauthorized and arbitrary act on my part.

Ironic Accident and Death

[continued from Our Southern Home February 8, 1900]

About the later part of November or first of December a very sad and unfortunate accident happened on the picket line. It was a beautiful moonlight night; about 10 or 11 o'clock I heard the sharp report of a gun on the picket line followed immediately by a loud cry. I knew someone had been shot. I had heard such a cry too often not to know what it meant. I ran as quick as I could to the spot and found J. P. Vann—known as Tobe Vann—of Co. A, writhing in pain and weltering in his blood on the sand of the beach. He was shot through the body by a minnie ball which passed through his bowels, which is the most painful of all wounds, so far as my observation goes. Upon investigation I ascertained that Vann and John Praytor occupied positions next to each other on the picket line, and in walking their respective beats, they met at the end of the line and stopped to talk a few minutes. Some one else came up about that time and Vann walked off and went to the end of his beat and turned to walk back. As I have stated it was a beautiful night, the moon shining brightly, so that every thing could be seen very distinctly for a considerable distance. Just as Vann turned to walk back to where Praytor and the other soldier stood, Praytor said, raising his gun to his shoulder, "now if he was a Yankee I could get him," and instantly the gun fired and Vann fell. No one was more surprised than Praytor; he and Vann were perfectly friendly at the time and, in fact, there had never been any trouble between them. Vann was one of the most amiable men in the company. No one seemed to regret the unfortunate occurrence more than Praytor. Poor fellow, he soon followed Vann, but the bullet that did the fatal work in his case sped from a gun in hostile hands. Vann died the next day and we buried him at a little church not far from The Village.

Gen. Liddell ordered Praytor's arrest, and charges preferred against him, but nothing ever came of it. No one believed that it was intentional but that he had cocked his gun involuntarily when he raised it to his shoulder, and pressed his finger against the trigger, not knowing that it was cocked. Or the hammer might have been knocked back in taking the gun from the stack and caught so that it was cocked and he might have been carrying it that way all night.

Poor Tobe, he was a good soldier and had passed through many battles and skirmishes, and it seemed hard that he should thus fall at the hands of a friend.

Our Southern Home February 22, 1900

As the fall came on the nights became quite cool, and a great many of the men had chills, and some few, had fever. The duties of picketing so long a line became onerous, as owing to so much sickness, the men who were well enough for duty, had to go on picket every night. In order to relieve us somewhat, Co. C, under Capt. Brunson was sent down to assist in picketing the line we had picketed since early August. They were located below us at Hollywood.

Spies Repulsed

[continued from <u>Our Southern Home</u> February 22, 1900]

One night while Lieut. Monette was with one group of his pickets, he thought he detected something moving on the water, and watching closely discovered that it was a small boat coming directly to the beach. Having his men concealed behind some drift wood lying on the beach, he waited until the boat was within a few feet of the beach, when they sprang out to seize the boat, in which were two or three men, but the enemy were too quick for them, and before Lieut. Monette and his men could reach the boat they were pulling out towards the Federal fleet with all their might. Lieut. Monette's men poured a volley into them, but whether any of those in the boat were struck or not, we never knew. It was very evident that their purpose was to land and let one or more of their number get ashore so as to get within our lines, and get information as to the strength of our forces, and where posted.

As winter approached we had some very cold weather; the men being thinly clad suffered considerably, as they were not allowed to build fires along the picket line. About the middle of December we were relieved and rejoined the regiment at Spanish Fort. The Federal fleet lay out in the Bay and in full view of our batteries. Occasionally a vessel would approach a little nearer than usual, when one of the big Columbiad guns in Battery Gladden, Huger, or Tracy would be turned loose shaking the marshy flats around like a small earthquake. These three batteries—Huger, Gladden and Tracy—were built at about equal distance from each other, on made ground, and then between these were obstructions made by driving piling down, the whole front being filled with torpedoes.

Whiskey Raid

[continued from Our Southern Home February 22, 1900]

On the night of Christmas eve the men learning that there was some whiskey in the Commissary Department, made a raid on the building and took it by force. Quite a number of Cos. A, C, and K—the Sumter County companies—were into this little affair, and as a result soon found themselves boarding at "Hotel Hitchcok," in Mobile, "Joseph Zimmerin, a Sergeant of the 22nd Louisiana, Proprietor in charge." Co. A was well represented in this squad of boarders, and some of them have a very "warm feeling" for their host Zimmerin, until this day.

About the first of Jan. 1865 we were transferred to the Mobile side of the bay. We were camped at the Magnolia Race Course on the Shell Road, some three miles from Mobile. We were not very comfortable here, as the houses were open, the weather very cold for that latitude, and with but little wood to cook with, or warm by in the open air, as the houses we occupied had no chimneys. Another cause of complaint was the short rations. Our meat was a very scanty supply of very poor beef, and a little corn meal. It is a remarkable fact, so far as my observation went during the war, that when any part of our army was in a section where it ought to have been well supplied, there was the greatest scarcity. This was the case at Vicksburg and all through the Mississippi campaign. Here at Mobile with the Mobile & Ohio R. R., the Alabama, Tombigby and Warrior rivers, all open and a large number of steamboats lying idle, there is no reason why there should not have been an abundance of meal, sweet potatoes, dried fruit, fresh pork, fat cattle and in fact almost everything needed by soldiers in camp, brought in either by water or rail. But the Commissary Department, one of the most important branches of the government, was badly managed throughout the entire war.

After remaining at Magnolia Race Course for ten days or two weeks we were ordered back to Spanish Fort. About this time the wrecks of the Army of Tennessee commenced passing through on their return from Gen. Hood's ill starred expedition into Tennessee. On the 28th of Jan. 1865, our brigade received orders to hold themselves in readiness to move at once. On the 29th, we were put on board a steamboat and started up the Alabama River for Montgomery, which we reached in about three days. From Montgomery we took the train for Columbus, Georgia, from there to Augusta. We were several days making this trip, as we had to walk a good part of the way, the railroad having been destroyed by Sherman in his march across the state.

To South Carolina

Our Southern Home April 26, 1900

We remained at Augusta only a day or two, when we were transferred to Hamburg on the South Carolina side of the Savannah River, where General Cheatham was collecting together the fragments of the Army of Tennessee as they arrived. We remained at Hamburg several days and then started on our journey across South Carolina. Having but few wagons and the railroads cut and destroyed by the enemy, the first thing we did was to discard all surplus baggage as we had to carry our rations and ammunition. Our articles of clothing, etc., thus left were packed in boxes and never seen by us again. Among other things I left a Bible that I had carried with me during the war. General Cheatham had collected together about two thousand men of different divisions, brigades and regiments. Our objective point was Columbia, the capital of South Carolina, hoping to reach that point and unite with the Confederate forces there before the enemy could get there. But in this we were foiled as they had succeeded in keeping a large force interposed between us and that place and forcing us to make a circuit to the west. Our first day's march was in the direction of Graniteville over sand beds like those near Gaston and in Sandtuck, and like that section of our county it was covered with post oak runners, black jack and a few hickory and pine trees. At Graniteville there was a factory of some kind, and the operatives, women and girls, came out to look at us as we passed along, as that was the first appearance of soldiers in so large a body in that section. As usual the boys had something to say as they passed along. If they could only hear a girl's name called that was all they wanted and down the line it would pass "Howdy Mary!" "I am glad to see you Mary," "Goodbye Mary," "How's your Ma, Mary" and so on until the poor girl would seek protection in flight.

From Graniteville we marched to Aiken that being the most direct route to Columbia, but here we deflected to the left, going in the direction of Newberry. The character of the country over which we passed had changed from sand to red clay hills. With the drenching rains of February falling upon us every day, and the roads terribly cut up by so much travel, made it anything but pleasant traveling. When we reached Newberry, Columbia had fallen and we remained there about a week awaiting developments. While walking with Lieu-

132

tenants Peteet and Knighton, the latter suggested that we go and call on Mrs. Higgins, whose son married a Miss Childs of Sumter, and had located in Butler, Choctaw County, to practice law prior to the war. She received us very cordially, and it being near dinner time she insisted that we remain for dinner, which we did, enjoying an elegant repast.

We found here two or three dozen ladies busily engaged in working for the soldiers. Some were making clothes, some knitting socks and some were scraping lint and preparing bandages for the wounded. Of all the places I soldiered during the war I found no place equal to South Carolina; nothing they had was too good for "our boys" as they called them. The loyalty and devotion of these women to the cause of the Confederacy was beautiful and sublime. Even when the dark clouds of adversity were hovering over the whole land and not a ray of hope penetrated their murky folds, these noble women were brave and hopeful; many of them had given up husbands, fathers and brothers, but no such word as surrender passed their lips.

When we returned to camp near the town we found the entire command on a train that had been made up out the odds and ends of cars that had been saved on that part of the road, and upon inquiry we ascertained that we were to meet a raid coming in the direction of a little place called Pomaria. General Cheatham had his men packed in and on the cars like sardines in a box. We soon started and were in a short distance of the place where we were to debark, when the car in front of us and the one in our rear ran off the track. A great many men were sitting on the top of these boxcars, Lieuts. Knighton, Peteet and myself among the number. I was sitting between them, and when the bumping of the cars indicated that they were off the track, they each started to jump, when I laid my hand on each and prevented their doing so. It was fortunate that I did so for nearly every one who jumped off was hurt—some quite severely. This was the nearest I ever came to being in an accident on a railroad. It was wonderful, considering the hundreds and hundreds of miles we traveled on trains during the war, with wornout rails, rotten cross ties and bridge timbers that no serious accident occurred. We soon learned that if there was a raid it had turned in another direction, and we returned to Newberry. The next day we started in the direction of Chester, a town situated on the line of railroad from Columbia to Charlotte, North Carolina. We crossed the French Broad River at night. It is a beautiful stream, and it was quite a picturesque scene as we were ferried over in long narrow boats that had been used in carrying ore down the river, the moon shining brightly, the shadows of the boats and men flitting back and forth over the surface of the beautiful river made a beautiful picture. After reaching Chester we had to wait a day or two for trains to be made up to take us to Charlotte and from thence to Raleigh.

A Month's Journey

[continued from Our Southern Home April 26, 1900]

So it will be seen that we were a month or more in going from Mobile, Alabama to Raleigh, North Carolina. But it must be born in mind that we had to march a good deal of the way in Georgia, and entirely across the state of South Carolina. But even when we had railroad transportation the rolling stock and road beds were in such condition, that ten or fifteen miles an hour was considered good speed.

Our Southern Home May 10, 1900

Baker's Brigade remained at Raleigh about twenty-four hours, encamped near the depot. On the platform of the depot there were a large number of barrels of whiskey, with guards all around to protect it from the depredation of the soldiers. But it took wide awake sentinels, and shrewd officers to foil an old soldier if he wanted a thing badly, especially if it was whiskey. Some one procured an auger, and some got buckets and crawling under the floor of the platform they proceeded to bore a hole through the floor and into one of the barrels, and filled their buckets with the much coveted liquid. As a result, before the officers knew of it nearly every man in the brigade was drunk, and some of the officers were in the same condition. Quite a number of the men went up town and proceeded to "take the town in," and ended by being themselves "taken in," and spent the night in the calaboose.

The brigade left early next morning leaving twenty-five, or thirty men and one or two officers, some of whom were in limbo and others who had straggled off, not knowing or caring when the brigade left. Adjutant C. H. Ellerbee and myself were detailed to remain behind and draw from the Quarter Master's Department Confederate gray cloth for officer's uniforms for our regiment. We obtained the cloth, and there being no train we had to remain in Raleigh that night. The next day we spent waiting patiently for a train which arrived late at night. In the sitting room of the depot were a large number of women who had come into the city that morning to sell butter, eggs, etc. and draw rations from the commissary, and every one of them without exception was bitter in denunciation of the Southern Confederacy, and especially the conscript law. It was the first time I had ever heard fall from the lips of a Southern woman anything but words of love and devotion for the Southern cause. It must be borne in mind however that they belonged to a class upon whom the war fell heavily in taking from them their husbands and fathers, and as they understood it, but little for them to fight for. While in Raleigh we ascertained that there were large supplies of sugar, coffee, rice, soap, meat, flour, tobacco and other articles in the Commissary Department belonging to the Confederate Government, while in the Quarter Master's Department was clothing, shoes and blankets in abundance, while the men were suffering for food, shoes and clothes. Nor was this confined to Raleigh but at other points in North Carolina and South Carolina the same was true, and when the surrender came most of it fell into the hands of the enemy. At Greensboro I saw hundreds of hogsheads of tobacco rolled out and every man who used the article could help himself to as much as he wanted.

There is no greater curse to an army then to have badly managed Commissary and Quarter Master's Departments. Napoleon shot a quartermaster every now and then for neglect of duty. The Confederacy needed some of Napoleon's discipline. Both of these departments were miserably managed, being often a refuge for relatives and friends, who speculated upon the wants of the soldiers in the field.

Battle of Bentonville

Leaving Raleigh late at night we arrived at Smithfield where the remnants of the Army of Tennessee were being collected together. We were placed in our former division—Clayton's—the corps being commanded by Lieut. Gen. Stewart. We remained near Smithfield until the morning of March the 18th when we received orders to move forward in the direction of Bentonville. We reached Bentonville late in the evening, and bivouacked for the night after a wearisome march of fifteen or sixteen miles.

Here we had the first glimpse of General Joe Johnston since he had been restored to command by General Lee. The men were wild with delight at seeing their beloved Commander again, and such love and devotion as they exhibited would have affected a much colder and less sympathetic man than General Johnston. He was visibly affected as he looked upon the remnants of worn and battle scarred veterans all that remained of that magnificent body of men he had left, but a few months before. Divisions were reduced to brigades, brigades to regiments and regiments to companies, their torn and tattered flags told of the strife through which they had passed. Though few in number they were prepared to give a good account of themselves. To many a poor fellow, this was the last night on earth; many an eye gazed at the stars overhead for the last time. Tomorrow was to witness the last struggle of any importance between the contending forces.[41]

For unknown reasons Judge Sprott did not finish this series in Our Southern Home. *However, at the insistence of his friend, T. M. Owen, Director of Archives and History, he wrote a "Sketch of the 40th Alabama" in August, 1906. This "Sketch," although more condensed, is basically the same material that he had written earlier. Since Judge Sprott includes the battle of Bentonville in this work, we are using it to complete his memoir.*

Gen. Joseph E. Johnston had been placed in Command by Gen. Lee, now Commander in Chief of the Confederate Armies, and was concentrating what forces he could get together to strike a blow at Sherman's army advancing on Goldsborough. Baker's Brigade was again placed in Clayton's Division. On the 18th of March the army moved out from Smithfield and camped near Bentonville. Early on the morning of the 19th, the men caught sight of Gen'l Johnston for the first time since they had seen him in Georgia. The men in the ranks did not know that the enemy was near and were not aware of it until they heard the familiar zip-zip of minnie balls. Clayton's Division was on the extreme right, that wing of the army being under Lieut. Gen'l Hardee. It took some time to get the different commands in position owing to the thick undergrowth. Stoval's Brigade occupied the front line just on the edge of an old field which had grown up in pines six or eight inches in diameter. About 2 o'clock, P.M. the enemy advanced through the old field at double quick; they were allowed to come within forty or fifty yards of Stoval's line before a shot was fired. The Confederates were lying down and the enemy did not see them; they evidently thought that it was nothing more than a cavalry picket with which they had been skirmishing that morning. But all at once a blaze shot out from Stoval's line from one end to the other. The slaughter was fearful; the ground was literally covered with the dead and wounded enemy. After this there was a lull, except pickets firing. In about an hour a single cannon boomed out from the center of our line, this was the signal for the advance. Baker's Brigade was now in front and swept forward and captured a strong line of redoubts. Rushing up the hill, they captured a strong line of works, some prisoners and two or three pieces of artillery. The Federals seemed panic stricken, and the field was covered with dead and wounded, discarded guns, blankets, knapsacks, and camp kettles filled with provisions. The knapsacks were large and bulky, and in them were found silk dresses, silver forks, spoons, jewelry, and in some of them were ladies' underclothing. These were some of Sherman's *gallant* soldiers who had marched through Georgia and South Carolina making war on women and children and noncombatants. The Confederates continued to advance; Baker's Brigade still in the front line. The last line of the enemy behind strong breast-works of large pine logs was struck, and carried by Baker's Brigade in their front, but a strong federal force appearing on our right flank, the order to fall back was given, but Lieut. Col. Gulley in command of the 40th Ala. failed to hear it so he with part of the regiment and colors passed over the works of the enemy on through their ammunition train, and finding that they were cut off went entirely around Sherman's army striking a railroad near Raleigh, and in a week or 10 days rejoined the command.[42] In this last charge the 40th Ala. lost heavily in killed and wounded, among the killed being Capt. Latham of Co. B and Clarence H. Ellerbee, Adjutant of the regiment.[43] The enemy had advanced so close to the right flank of the 40th that in falling back several officers and men were captured, among them Capt. Campbell and Lieut. Williams of Co. D, Lieut. Hall of Co. A and Lieut. Thomas of Co. C. There was perhaps never a greater display of flags upon any one battlefield, than was displayed by the Army of Tennessee. Brigades had been reduced to the size of regiments, and regiments to that of companies, and this brought the flags close together. There was no more gallant and desperate fighting during the war than was done by this little army of Confederates at the Battle of Bentonville. On the field were Gen'ls Johnston, Beauregard and Bragg, and Lieut. Gen'ls Hardee and Stewart and a large number of major generals. As the men went into the fight, you could hear on all sides "Boys let's fight one more battle for old Joe." Although almost every man in the ranks knew that the end was near yet they were willing to sacrifice their lives for the general they loved.

About sundown the firing ceased and both armies rested in the positions they occupied. On Monday March 20th, 1865, skirmishing was kept up along the whole line. Sherman was concentrating his forces as fast as he could, and on Tuesday, the 21st, made the effort to turn the left of the Confederate forces, but in this they were foiled. Baker's Brigade was double quicked from the extreme right to the extreme left where the enemy were met and kept in check until dark put an end to the conflict. Here the 40th Ala. performed its last duty upon the battlefield; the picket line covering the brigade was from the 40th under Command of Lieut. Sprott, the entire picket line being under Gen'l Walthall. The orders were to hold the line until daylight, and then fall back and follow the army, which had fallen back during the night. It was after sunrise when the pickets were relieved and those of Baker's Brigade arrived at the bridge over Mill Creek, the only avenue of escape, just as the rear of the Confederate cavalry was crossing. The enemy did not pursue and after a day's rest the army moved to the railroad near Smithfield. (Baker's Brigade is credited with capturing 204 prisoners at Bentonville, but an accompanying note says this report is not reliable. See Serial 100, page 687. From page 734, ib., The 40th Alabama was commanded, March 31st,

1865, by Captain Thomas M.. Brunson.) While at or near Smithfield the Army of Tennessee was reorganized—the regiments and brigades being so reduced as to require them to be consolidated. The 40th Ala. was consolidated with the 19th Ala. and the consolidated regiment was know as the 19th Ala. Col. Mike L. Woods of the 46th became colonel. E.S. Gulley of the 40th Ala. became lieut. col., and E. D. Willett of the 40th became major. Lieut. J. Wesley Johnson of Co. F, 40th Ala. became adjutant. The 19th was placed in the brigade of Gen'l Pettus—Major Gen'l Stevenson's Division. The army fell back to Raleigh and from there to Greensboro, N.C. From there Pettus' Brigade was sent to Salisbury to meet a raid of cavalry. They arrived in time to save the railroad bridge over the Yadkin River, but not in time to save the public stores at Salisbury. The surrender of Gen'l Johnston soon after took place and on May 4th, 1865, paroles were issued to Pettus' Brigade, and on the next day they took up their sacks and wearily journeyed homeward.[44]

Appendix

&

Notes

Appendix

Moore's Brigade, Maury's Division
Army of the West
Later known as
Baker's Brigade, Stewart's Division
Army of Tennessee

Colonel John C. Moore of the 2nd Texas Infantry Regiment was appointed Brigadier General on May 26th, 1862. He received command of a brigade in Maury's Division, Army of the West, which served in Mississippi until after the fall of Vicksburg. Moore nominated two officers for his staff by August 1, 1862:

Maurice K. Simmons	Commissary
James W. Magnum	Assistant Adjutant General

Initially no Alabama units belonged to this brigade. However, by the end of August, Portis's 42nd Alabama Infantry Regiment had joined. During the campaign in Mississippi, which included the battles of Iuka (September 19th, 1862) and Corinth (October 3-5 1862), Moore's Brigade appeared as follows:

42nd Alabama Infantry Regiment	Colonel John W. Portis
15th Arkansas Infantry Regiment	Colonel Squire Boone
23rd Arkansas Infantry Regiment	Lieutenant Colonel A.A. Pennington
2nd Texas Infantry Regiment	Colonel W.P. Rogers
35th Mississippi Infantry Regiment	Colonel William S. Barry
Missouri Battery	Captain Hiram M. Bledsoe

By October 20th, 1862, Bledsoe's Missouri battery and the Arkansas regiments had been ordered elsewhere replaced by the 37th Alabama Infantry Regiment. The 40th Alabama and the 40th Mississippi Infantry Regiments were added to General Moore's Brigade at the end of 1862. The following regiments participated in the defense of Vicksburg as part of Moore's command:

37th Alabama Infantry Regiment	Colonel James F. Dowdell
40th Alabama Infantry Regiment	Lieutenant Colonel John H. Higley
42nd Alabama Infantry Regiment	Colonel John W. Portis
35th Mississippi Infantry Regiment	Colonel William S. Barry
40th Mississippi Infantry Regiment	Colonel Wallace B. Colbert
2nd Texas Infantry Regiment	Colonel Ashbel Smith

Officers and men of General Moore's Brigade surrendered with Forney's Division at Vicksburg, Mississippi, July 4, 1863. Receiving paroles within a few days, they soon reassembled at Demopolis, Alabama. The Mississippi and Texas units were reassigned, which left only three Alabama regiments in the brigade. By the end of October 1863, these reported to the

Army of Tennessee outside Chattanooga, Tennessee, becoming part of Cheatham's Division.

General Moore left the army after the fighting at Chattanooga to resign February 3, 1864. Colonel John H. Higley of the 40th Alabama then led the brigade as its senior officer. Meanwhile, Colonel Alpheus Baker of the 54th Alabama Infantry Regiment was appointed Brigadier General to rank March 5, 1864, assuming command of Moore's Brigade two weeks later. Baker's 54th Alabama was relieved at Montgomery, Alabama, April 28, 1864, and attached to the brigade. Serving in the division commanded by Generals A.P. Stewart and H.D. Clayton, Baker's Brigade included these regiments during the Atlanta Campaign:

37th Alabama Infantry Regiment	Lieutenant Colonel Alex A. Greene
40th Alabama Infantry Regiment	Colonel John H. Higley
42nd Alabama Infantry Regiment	Lieutenant Colonel Thomas C. Lanier
54th Alabama Infantry Regiment	Lieutenant Colonel John A. Minter

General Baker nominated the following staff members:

Philip Allen Sapp	Commissary
Waites E. Gibbs	Quartermaster
James M. Loughborough	Assistant Adjutant General
Hugh M. Pollard	Assisstant Inspector General
Joseph F. Dennis	Aide-de-Camp

Before the fall of Atlanta, Baker's Brigade was relieved and ordered to Mobile, Alabama. His Alabama regiments remained in the defenses of that city until January 28, 1865. On that date the command was directed to return to the Army of Tennessee, moving via Montgomery en route to Augusta, Georgia. During its stay at Mobile, other units were attached to the depleted brigade:

37th Alabama Infantry Regiment	
40th Alabama Infantry Regiment	Colonel John H. Higley
42nd Alabama Infantry Regiment	
54th Alabama Infantry Regiment	Captain Charles C. McCall
3rd Alabama Reserve Battalion	
4th Alabama Reserve Battalion	Lieutenant Colonel E. M. Underhill
22nd Louisiana Infantry Regiment	

The Army of Tennessee reorganized on April 9, 1865, and Brigadier General William F. Brantley was assigned the consolidated regiments of Deas's, Manigualt's, Sharp's, Baker's, and Brantley's Brigades. The survivors of Baker's Brigade surrendered May 1, 1865, at Greensboro, North Carolina. Evidently General Baker returned to his home just prior to the surrender.

Notes

1. The victories of Forts Henry and Donaldson by Brigadier General Ulysses S. Grant shattered the defensive line that Confederate General A.S. Johnston hoped would hold northern Tennessee and Kentucky.

2. On October 3rd and 4th, 1862 General Earl Van Dorn, with a force of 10,000 men, moved north to join and even larger body of troops numbering 17,000 led by Sterling Price. Together, they attacked a Union supply depot in Corinth, Mississippi.

The initial assault on October 3rd, by Van Dorn's three divisions, was successful in driving the Yankees out of their primary earthworks. Nightfall prevented further Confederate attacks.

On the morning of the 4th, Van Dorn ordered his troops to resume the attack. Spearheaded by the 2nd Texas Infantry Regiment, the Confederates were successful in breaking the Union defensive position but ran into devastating volleys by Rosecrans' reserves. The battle was over by noon with the Confederates hobbling away.

3. *Battle of Chickasaw Bayou* On December 20th, 1862 Sherman launched one of the largest amphibious assaults of the war. He hoped that his force of 40,000 infantry would be able to carry out Grant's orders to move down the Mississippi River and land at the point where the Yazoo River emptied into the Mississippi just above Vicksburg. From this point he was to cut all railroad supply lines and begin siege operations.

Sherman's advance was halted on December 27th. His army had landed at Johnston's Plantation north of Vicksburg. He attacked three Confederate divisions under Major General Martin Smith, whose lines sat atop well-fortified positions on Walnut Hills. Smith's front was covered by Chickasaw Bayou, which was crossable in only a few places. Sherman's line of attack was restricted to a three-mile stretch of the Confederate works, these being bordered on the Confederate right by Thompson's Lake and on the left by the Mississippi. Smith was outnumbered by Sherman almost two to one, but with Smith's troops so well entrenched this did not matter.

Sherman initiated the action by sending skirmishers forward on December 27th to probe the Confederate line. He followed suit on the 28th. On the morning of the 29th he began the preparatory bombardment that lasted two hours. He then ordered the doomed infantry assaults forward. Sherman oversaw five separate assaults: each failed. The action of the 29th cost him 2,000 men, while the Confederates lost 127.

Sprott mentions Brigadier General Stephen D. Lee as having a conspicuous part in the battle. The brunt of Sherman's assaults fell on Lee's front, and he was heavily engaged for almost the entire day on the 29th.

4. *Sherman's Advance Up Little Deer Creek* On March 16th, 1863, Grant ordered Sherman to take part of the Federal 15th corps and move up Steele's Bayou. Sherman would again be assisted by a naval force under Rear Admiral David Porter comprised of five ironclads, four mortar boats,

and two tugs. The mission ran into trouble quickly. With Sherman's troops on tugs, Porter's Ironclads and mortar boats led the flotilla. The ships had pass obstacles that Confederate defenders had put in the water. Logs and other floating debris also hampered progress; low-hanging limbs knocked smokestacks and men off the ships. Confederate snipers kept up an aggravating fire that slowed forward movement even further until the flotilla averaged four miles every twenty-four hours. Porter's advance was stopped completely by a barge that Confederates had sunk to block the channel. Porter also received intelligence that Confederates were bringing up artillery to force capitulation.

Sherman moved his troops up quickly to aid Porter. Arriving in time to meet the first column of Confederate infantry that had been dispatched to capture the fleet, Sherman held off the Confederate column long enough for Porter to extract his ships and retreat back to Steele's Bayou. Porter had to back his ships down the small channel to make good his escape.

5. Stone's Battalion Companies A, D, and I of the 40th Alabama were detached from the regiment and put under the command of Major Thomas O. Stone. The detachment was dubbed "Stone's Battalion" and quickly marched up the Yazoo and then up the Sunflower River to act as scouts for Pemberton's main body of troops situated in and around Vicksburg.

While Stone's Battalion was conducting operations, Grant's final push on Vicksburg was successful in driving the city's defenders into its trenches. Grant had accomplished almost total encirclement of the Confederate defenses, and the two sides settled into a siege.

"Stone's Battalion" was now orphaned from the rest of the 40th. Stone took his force to Rolling Fork to pick up sick and wounded men that the 40th had to leave behind, in their haste to get back to Vicksburg. With that accomplished, Stone moved the battalion to Greenwood, which, in the spring, was a hard, muddy march. At Greenwood they were ordered to join General Joseph E. Johnston's army that was concentrating in an effort to link up with Pemberton's besieged men.

Under Johnston's command, Stone's Battalion would participate in the action at Jackson in a brigade commanded by Brigadier General Matthew D. Ector. The battalion would stay with Ector's Brigade of Major General W.H.T. Walker's division until just prior to the battles for Chattanooga. Following the action at Jackson, Walker's Division was ordered to Bragg's army and would be heavily engaged at the Battle of Chickamauga.

6. Vicksburg Surrendered Pemberton surrendered the city of Vicksburg to Grant on July 4th, 1863. After forty-eight days of shelling and near starvation, Pemberton felt that a continuation of hostilities was futile. The entire garrison was taken prisoner and quickly paroled.

7. Battle of Jackson With the situation in Vicksburg worsening everyday, General Joseph E. Johnston was sent to Mississippi. Johnston moved his force into the city of Jackson and quickly ascertained that the defensive works around the city were less than adequate for withstanding a Federal offensive. Johnston ordered a retreat to the city of Canton but left four brigades behind, under General John Gregg, to hold out until supplies and state records could be evacuated. Johnston told Gregg that once everything had been taken out to move his four brigades to Canton.

Federal assaults began on May 14th, 1863 amidst rainy conditions. Confederate resistance was slight at best but Gregg lost some 900 casualties.

By not staying to hold the city, Johnston denied Pemberton the possibility of attacking the Federal rear and ultimately linking the two commands. This was the last chance for the Vicksburg garrison to be reinforced. The retreat allowed Grant to swing the full weight of his army towards Pemberton.

8. *Ringgold, GA; Longstreet's movements* Longstreet's Corps had been detached from Lee's Army of Northern Virginia on September 6th, 1863. The corps was forced to take a southern detour that nearly doubled their travel time. The first of Longstreet's men, John Bell Hood's Division, arrived on September 17th, 1863 in Ringgold, GA. Bragg postponed his advance on the enemy for one more day.

9. *Chickamauga Scientifically fought* History would disagree with Sprott's statement that the great battle of Chickamauga was "one of the most scientifically fought battles . . . during the Civil War." In actuality, the battle seemed to be more a confused fistfight than a clean and tactically executed battle. The two-day melee was a continuous mistake with each general capitalizing, or not capitalizing, on his enemy's blunders.

10. *Casualty Figures* With Longstreet's reinforcements from Vurginia, Bragg's Army of Tennessee numbered approximately 66,000 men by the 18th of September, and Rosecrans's Army of the Cumberland numbered some 58,000. This was one of the very few battles in which the Confederates enjoyed a slight advantage in numbers. By the night of September 19th, 1863 the Confederates had lost over 18,000 men and the Federals over 16,000.

11. *Eastern Rebs vs. Western Federals* When Longstreet's veterans for the Army of Northern Virginia moved from Virginia to Bragg's aid in Tennessee, the meeting between Eastern Theater Confederates and Western Theatre Confederates was a very interesting one. As the Veterans of Virginia marched past the men of the west, the latter were struck by the uniformity of the easterners and the superior equipage that they carried. On the other hand, Longstreet's men marched past the westerners with an air of contempt. It was much the picture of the planter's son meeting the tough backwoodsman.

The Eastern Confederates looked forward to taking care of these Western Theatre Yankees as handily as they had the Federals up north. Just as Sprott mentions, the Eastern Confederates soon learned that they were fighting a different kind of Union soldier and he wouldn't run as easily.

12. *What was Ector's Brigade doing?* It would be an understatement to say that Ector's Brigade was heavily engaged in the battle of Chickamauga. The brigade was part of Major General W.H.T. Walker's Reserve Corps.

Ector's Brigade spent September 18th, 1863 trying with the rest of Walker's command to force a crossing of Chickamauga Creek at Alexander's Bridge. Walker began his initial attack at approximately noon. John T. Wilder's Federal "Lightning" brigade of mounted infantry held for over four hours. But when the cavalry on his left flank, under Colonel Robert H. G. Minty, began to retire, Wilder knew it was time to fall back. His troops left the bridge in ruins and retreated just ahead of Confederate pursuers.

With the bridge destroyed, Walker marched the corps to Lambert's Ford, where they were successful in crossing the Chickamauga. Walker's men encamped after getting across the creek.

On the morning of September 19th, 1863, Ector's Brigade was sent forward to support Colonel Claudius Wilson's brigade. Walker had lent Wilson's brigade to Major General Nathan B. Forrest, who sent Wilson to attack the right flank of Federal Colonel John Croxton's brigade. Wilson pushed Croxton, but Colonel G. F. Dibrell's brigade of Tennessee dismounted cavalry was halted by a wall of fire.from Colonel Ferdinand Van Derveer's infantry brigade. Forrest commandeered Ector's Brigade to bolster Dibrell's attack. A crashing volley from Van Derveer's regiments also met this brigade. Without any artillery support, Ector was forced to retreat. The fighting continued until 11:00 am. Ector halted his brigade in the area around Jay's mill until approximately sundown. They would not be further engaged.

On September 20th, 1863, Ector's brigade was in Lieutenant General Leonidas Polk's wing, which encompassed the entire right flank of General Bragg's army. Bragg's battle plan for that day called for an attack en echelon from right to left. The attack was to be initiated by Polk's rightmost regiment and continue down the line until the Federals were blocked from getting to Chattanooga. With the brunt of the fighting falling on the front of Major General John C. Breckenridge's Division, Ector's brigade had limited involvement in the action of September 20th.

13. What battery? The battery of artillery that Sprott so vividly recounts attacking was a combined battery of the 4th U.S. Regular Artillery, Battery I, under the command of Lieutenant Frank Smith, and the First Michigan Light Artillery Battery D, under the command of Captain Josiah Church.

There appear to be time discrepancies in Sprott's narrative. The heaviest portion of fighting in which Ector's Brigade was involved would have been on the morning of the 19th of September. After being repulsed by the battery and its supporting infantry units, Ector pulled his beat-up brigade back to Jay's Mill Road around eleven o'clock in the morning and held them in reserve for the rest of the day. The fact is that Ector's Brigade had been cut to pieces, and there was no way that his men could take the offensive. Cheatham's Division came to aid Walker and took over the attack. This division, too, was repulsed with heavy loss, and the Yankees remained in control of the Winfrey Field. At dusk, Major General Patrick R. Cleburne and his crack division passed through the shattered commands of Walker and Cheatham. Bragg ordered Cleburne to take his troops and push the Yankees back. The task would prove to be a daunting one in the gathering darkness.

14. The Hardee Pattern Battle flag The flag referred to as the Hardee Pattern battle flag consists of a blue field bordered in white tape with a white disc in the center. Confederate General Simon Bolivar Buckner designed the flag so that he might easily be able to identify his troops on the field of battle. General Hardee adopted the flag when he organized his corps in 1862. Despite widespread adoption, in the western army, of the Army of Northern Virginia pattern battle flag, Cleburne's men refused to turn over their distinctive banners. Even the Federal soldiers knew that if they saw the blue flags of Cleburne's Division, it meant hard licks.

15. *Patrick Royanne Cleburne* One of only two foreign born officers to attain the rank of Major General, Cleburne was born in County Cork, Ireland. Before emigrating to the United States, Cleburne served a three-year enlistment in Her Majesty's 41st Regiment of Foot. When he arrived in this country, in 1849, he first lived in Cincinnati as an apothecary but soon relocated to Helena, Arkansas. In Arkansas, Cleburne studied law while maintaining a partnership in a drugstore. By the outbreak of war in 1861, Cleburne had built a fine reputation as a lawyer and he had accumulated considerable amounts of property. He left civilian life behind him when he raised the 15th Arkansas Infantry Regiment, of which he was elected Colonel. Cleburne received his promotion to Brigadier General on March 4th, 1862.

Cleburne led his brigade at the Battle of Shiloh, April, 1862, and also at Perryville and Richmond. He rapidly gained the reputation of being a very talented combat officer. He was promoted to Major General on December 16th, 1862. Cleburne became known as the "Stonewall Jackson of the West" to his soldiers and his many civilian admirers.

16. *Description of Cleburne's night assault* This attack made by Major General Patrick R. Cleburne's division was, ultimately, a waste of lives. A night attack, in any war, is a risky venture.

On the evening of September 19th, 1863, after repeated attacks by the divisions of Benjamin Cheatam and W.H.T. Walker had failed to push the Federal left flank to the south, Bragg ordered Lieutenant Daniel Harvey Hill to send Cleburne's division to help in the effort. Cleburne's troops, three brigades under Brigadier Generals S.A.M. Wood, Lucius Polk, and James Desheler, were formed in a front. Cleburne placed Wood's brigade in the center with Polk on the right and Desheler on the left. Cleburne's only command to his brigadiers was to guide on the center (Wood) and move as quickly as possible—any battery encountered was to be taken.

The battle, overall, became too reckless. Many of the Confederates stopped firing for fear of shooting down their comrades in the darkness. The assault sputtered to a halt. Cleburne's famous division had driven the Federals from their positions around Winfrey field, back to Thomas' main line, near the Lafayette road. Cleburne could only claim Winfrey field as his prize. The bodies of the men who had fallen in the fight for the field earlier in the day were now joined by the freshly slain of Cleburne's command.

17. *Federal Army Demoralized* Following the defeat of Rosecrans' army at Chickamauga, the Federals were basically routed. This was the first time the Army of the Cumberland had ever experienced such a disorganized

retreat.

Nathan Bedford Forrest, scouting ahead of the Army of Tennessee, called on Bragg repeatedly for a force of troops to exploit the situation and destroy the Federal Army on the night of September 20th. Bragg, unaware that there was no longer any enemy threat and fully expecting a renewal of the battle on September 21st, declined to send Forrest men.

18. *Why a Fruitless Victory?* The Battle of Chickamauga was the Army of Tennessee's only major victory of the war. Though they won the battle, the cost was heavy. Instead of issuing orders for an offensive action to finish off the badly beaten Federals, Braxton Bragg took time to reorganize. This gave Rosecrans time to build up the defenses around Chattanooga and make their position untenable to a large-scale Confederate assault.

Though prodded by Richmond to initiate forward movement, Bragg settled into temporary siege positions atop the heights of Lookout Mountain, endeavoring to starve his enemy into submission. Bragg's ineffective leadership and the worst command controversy of the war paralyzed the Army of Tennessee. The Confederates were not even successful in sealing off Federal supply routes that eventually saved the besieged Federal army when used by Grant and Hooker. Bragg's mishandling of affairs, coupled with the Confederate defeats of Lookout Mountain and Missionary Ridge, essentially erased the victory at Chickamauga and hope for a resounding Confederate victory in the west.

19. *Willett and Curry's Diaries* As Sprott states, this chapter is taken almost word for word from the diary of E.D.Willett. Willett was captain of company B, 40th Alabama Infantry Regiment. He faithfully recorded the movements of company B and the 40th Alabama from the day the regiment was mustered into service until his promotion in October 1864.

In order to produce a regimental history for company B, another diarist in the company, Sergeant John H. Curry, reinforced Willett's diary. Together, the diaries were published as a history of company B and the 40th Alabama, entitled *History of Company B (originally Picken's Planters) 40th Alabama Regiment Confederate States Army 1862-1865.* Colonial Press published the history, which is full of useful information.

20. *Battle of Baker's Creek or Champion Hill* In an attempt to cut Grant's lines of communications and position his troops in the rear of the Federal army, Pemberton sent three divisions forward to strike the Federals at Champion Hill on May 16th, 1863. The three division commanders—John S. Bowen, Carter L. Stevenson, and William Loring—were beaten and bloodied by Federal Infantry under Generals John Logan and Marcellus Crocker.

21. *On What Terms did Vicksburg Surrender?* Initially, Grant called for the unconditional surrender of Vicksburg (he couldn't disappoint the newspapers). Pemberton responded saying that unless Grant was willing to agree to terms, "You will bury many more of your men before you enter Vicksburg." Grant agreed to talk. Under the terms of the surrender, Confederate soldiers had to give up their arms but would be paroled and allowed to leave the city. Officers were allowed to retain their side arms, clothing, and one horse

each.

22. *Pemberton Controversy* Pemberton fell into controversy when many southerners accused him of being a traitor for surrendering on the 4th of July. He claimed he did so in an effort to achieve better terms. Pemberton blamed Johnston for the loss of the city by not making a more determined effort to reinforce the beleaguered defenders. Nevertheless, Pemberton accepted a reduction in rank and finished the war in the eastern theatre in relative obscurity.

Though Pemberton was a Pennsylvania native, it has to be seen that he was a devoted soldier for the south. Without proper reinforcements, the siege was just a matter of time. Pemberton fought hard, and it is to his credit that he stopped further bloodshed when he knew it would only be in vain.

23. *Moore's Report in the O.R.* When reunited, the 40th Alabama was brigaded with the 37th and 42nd Alabama Infantry Regiments under the command of Brigadier General John C. Moore. Moore's after-action report surrounding the action at Lookout Mountain and Missionary Ridge can be found in the Army Official Records of the War of the Rebellion, Series I Volume XXXI/2 (S#55).

24. *Orchard Knob Offensive* Major General George Thomas' corps of Chickamauga fame conducted this attack. Thomas attacked with three divisions under Brigadier General Thomas J. Wood, Major General Philip Sheridan, and Brigadier General Absalom Baired. Thomas' mission was to conduct a reconnaissance in force toward Orchard Knob to see if the Confederate positions were still occupied. It was left to Thomas' discretion on whether to seize Orchard Knob or not.

On the morning of November 23rd, Thomas' men moved out of the Chattanooga defenses. Confederates watching from Lookout thought that the Federal divisions were having a dress parade and marveled, impressed by the precision with which the enemy marched and formed their lines. The reality of the scene set in when a signal gun fired to announce the beginning of the attack. The Confederates jumped behind their works, and the skirmishers out in front of Orchard Knob ran back to the main line. When Thomas' men reached Orchard Knob, it was literally a matter of minutes before the attack was over. Thomas' men had established a beachhead from which an offensive against Lookout Mountain could be made.

Grant was pleased with the attack, he said, "This movement secured to us a line fully a mile in advance of the one we occupied in the morning."

25. *Cleburne's Defense of the Right Flank* Although Lieutenant General William J. Hardee was put in charge of the Confederate right flank, Hardee left the responsibility to his most trusted subordinate, Major General Patrick Cleburne. Cleburne was ordered by Hardee on the 24th of November to take his division and set up a defensive position at Tunnel Hill, the extreme right flank of Bragg's position. Thus ordered, Cleburne rode ahead of his advancing division to the tunnel where the Chattanooga and Cleveland Railroad passes through Missionary Ridge. This portion of the ridge is named Tunnel Hill.

Cleburne initially had just three brigades with which to guard Tunnel Hill. No matter how he constructed his line, the most important factor was for its extreme left to connect with Major General W.H.T. Walker's division. Cleburne sent Major Poole, one of Hardee's aides to inform Hardee that he had only three brigades to defend the position with. The moment Poole dashed away, Cleburne could see skirmishers of Major General William T. Sherman's command heading towards the ridge. With the eye of a skilled soldier, he began making dispositions. He directed James Smith's Texas brigade to hold the top of the hill. Smith put his brigade in line of battle facing north, with his right regiment facing east to protect his flank. Smith had scarcely thrown out a skirmish line before the skirmishers of Sherman's attacking force hit him.

Cleburne initially placed the brigade of Mark Lowrey south of the tunnel. He was about to place Daniel Govan's brigade on Lowrey's left so as to complete the connection with Walker's right flank ¾ of a mile away, when his attention was drawn to the volume of fire coming from the right of Smith's command. Knowing that the Yankees were attempting to turn his flank. Cleburne ordered Lowrey and Govan to meet the threat.

The Federal skirmishers kept up an annoying fire while Cleburne hastened to make his dispositions. When the firing stopped and evening descended over the ridge, Cleburne had Smith's brigade in the center of his line facing north. Govan was on Smith's right, facing slightly east. Hardee arrived on Tunnel Hill that evening and approved Cleburne's position. The only change he made was to take two regiments from Lowrey's brigade and place them on the detached spur to the front of Govan. The two regiments fronted to the west to strengthen an enfilade fire on any enemy attacks. By taking this detatchment from Lowrey's brigade, the link up with General Walker's right was impossible. The Confederates spent the night with a large gap in their line.

Sherman was supposed to attack early in the morning on the 25th, yet did not begin his assault until mid-morning. It seemed that Sherman was not living up to his reckless reputation. Sherman's delay bothered Grant, and the commanding general sent Sherman dispatches urging him to undertake the advance. By Grant's plan, Sherman should have attacked the enemy position at 6:30 a.m. It was not until approximately 10:30 a.m. that Sherman finally ordered the brigades of Corse and Loomis of his brother-in-law Hugh Ewing's division forward.

Sherman had every opportunity to overwhelm Cleburne; he commanded six divisions totaling 26,000 men against Cleburne, whose three brigades totalled just 10,000. Sherman's attacks were not coordinated, and weak considering the type of terrain his men had to cross. The Federal soldiers had to maneuver through ravines, open fields, and a ridge before they could even make contact with Cleburne's command. What the Confederates lacked in numbers, they made up for in their chosen defensive position.

On the morning of the 25th, Cleburne began receiving reinforcements. Just after sunrise, John Brown's Tennessee brigade arrived. It was placed between Smith's left and the tunnel. Brown threw out a skirmish line into the fields at the base of the ridge, known to locals as the flat. They held a line a bit north of the railroad tracks to the west of the ridge. On Brown's right, Cleburne placed the batteries of Calvert and Goldthwaite directly above the tunnel. The guns were trained to help Brown's brigade enfilade the approach to Tunnel Hill from the flat.

About 9:30 a.m. the brigade of Alfred Cummings arrived. Cleburne placed the 39th Georgia, of that brigade, to the left of Brown's brigade. Approximately the same time, General Joseph Lewis' famous Kentucky (Orphan) brigade arrived. Lewis was instructed to hold his men in reserve behind Smith's brigade.

Besides having guns above the tunnel, Cleburne placed two more batteries at crucial spots in his line. To bolster Smith's center, Cleburne ordered Swett's Mississippi battery to that spot. James P. Douglas' Texas battery was positioned in the center of Govan's brigade, in an effort to put enfilading fire on any enemy attacks coming on Smith's front.

When the brigades of Corse and Loomis set out to hit Cleburne's line, they focused on the position held by Smith's Texans. Smith's center pointed forward, forming a type of salient. The attackers used this position to guide on. The Confederates held their fire until the Yankees were very close, and then unleashed a volley of artillery and musketry that caused the Union line to quiver but not halt. Corse pressed the attack and soon Smith's salient came under a galling crossfire from the two brigades.

Those involved in the struggle stated that this was one of the most furious fights they had experienced. The gunners of Swett's Mississippi Battery, under the command of Lieutenant H. Shannon, felt the brunt of the firing. Amidst a continuous roar of musketry the artillerymen continued to work their guns. The ranks became so depleted that the highest-ranking survivor was a corporal and infantrymen had to be detailed to man the four twelve-pounder Napoleons.

The attack was finally beaten back when two of Smith's regiments jumped over the breastworks and slammed into the tired Federals, pushing them back. Corse fell in this assault, badly wounded, as did James Smith. Colonel Hiram Granbury took command of the Texas brigade in Smith's absence.

This offensive typified the fighting on the right flank on November 25th. All along Cleburne's line Federal soldiers were able to reach the Confederate positions only to be bloodily repulsed by concentrated infantry and artillery fire. The battle continued until 3:00 p.m. At that time, Cleburne was approached by Lieutenant Colonel E. Warfield and told that the men were wasting precious ammunition and that they were becoming disheartened at the persistence of the enemy. Warfield proposed a bayonet charge on the attackers. Of the suggestion Cleburne said, "I immediately consented, and directed General Cumming to prepare for the charge." Suddenly the fight became a large scale Little Round Top in reverse. Cleburne also directed a Texas Regiment to make a simultaneous attack on the Federal right flank. The counterattack succeeded despite dogged Federal resistance. Cleburne's men captured eight flags and five hundred prisoners; he lost fifty-two killed, one hundred and seventy-eight wounded, and two missing, out of his three brigades.

Cleburne summed up enemy loss in his official report, saying, "The enemy must have suffered severely, the hillside and the valley were thickly strewn with his dead, and if we pay credit his published reports of casualties in this fight, he lost one major general, John E. Smith, wounded; three brigadier generals, Corse, Matthies, and Giles Smith, wounded the latter mortally, and one colonel commanding brigade, Colonel Raum, mortally wounded."

While the defense of the right flank had been a complete success, the center of the Confederate line, on Missionary Ridge, had collapsed and the Army of Tennessee was in full retreat. Cleburne was ordered by Hardee to fall back of the Chickamauga and move to Chickamauga Station. The retreat was skillfully conducted and by 9:00 p.m. Cleburne's troops had left Tunnel Hill.

Cleburne's report of this action may be found in the Official Records, Series I Volume XXXI/2 (S#55).

26. *Crumbling of the left wing in the OR* Reference to the crumbling of Bragg's left flank can be found in the Official Records. The reports of Brigadier General John C. Moore, commanding the 37th, 40th, and 42nd Alabama regiments is located in Series I Volume XXXI/2 (S#55). The report of Brigadier General John K. Jackson, temporarily commanding Cheatem's division on Lookout Mountain, is also found in Volume XXXI/2 (S#55).

In his report, General Moore mentions his commander, General Jackson, as being too far to the rear to properly conduct division dispositions, while his command was involved in the fighting around the Craven's House. These accusations brought about questions as to Jackson's fortitude in battle forcing Jackson to write a lengthy report of the engagement on Lookout.

Jackson defends his tarnished reputation in that report by explaining his every move while his division was engaged near the Craven's House.

27. *Retreat of the left flank over Chickamauga Creek* A collapse of the Confederate center amidst Federal attacks on Missionary Ridge allowed Union troops to exploit a gap and fire on the rear of the Confederate position. With their position thus exposed, General Frank Cheatham's division had to first fend off the subsequent assaults and then find a way to extract his troops.

Moore's brigade and the 40th Alabama, now threatened in their front and rear, remained intact as did Walthall's brigade. This is quite a compliment to those units considering the losses they had sustained over the two days of fighting.

The other brigade in the division was John Jackson's, composed of regiments from Georgia and Mississippi regiments. Cheatham focused his attention on the fight developing on the left flank. He ordered Moore and Jackson's brigades out of their breastworks and to change front to the left so as to bring enfilading fire on the right regiments of Union General Absalom Baird's attacking division. As the enemy got closer, Jackson's brigade began to waver. With the first volley from Union Colonel Edward Phelp's brigade, Jackson's troops broke. The brigade scattered; many of the men ran through the ranks of Moore's brigade that were coming on line to Jackson's left in support.

Jackson, after a very difficult few minutes, was able to rally his men and bring them back into the line on Moore's right. The two united brigades formed a seemingly strong position that, in the waning light, looked very formidable. A volley from Moore's brigade and the loss of light finally halted Federal attacks. The Yankees never knew how close they were to bringing disaster upon the Army of Tennessee. Once Federal assaults ceased, Cheatham looked to the withdrawal of his division and directed his officers to lead their brigades over South Chickamauga Creek. He had two of his brigades (Walthall and Brown) throw out skirmish lines to cover the division's retreat. Once the main body was safe from any real threat, he told Walthall and Brown to take up the march.

Cheatham's personal direction of the retreat was a great comfort to his officers and the rank and file. The division crossed the creek without incident and reached Chickamauga Station, Bragg's rallying point, safely.

The rest of Hardee's Corps executed similarly skillful withdrawals, and by 9:00 p.m. the whole army had escaped annihilation. From Chickmauga Station, Bragg's army marched to Dalton, Georgia, where it would spend the winter of 1863-64.

28. *Sherman's conduct of the campaign* Sprott's description of Sherman's strategy outlines the essence of his plan. When Sherman felt Johnston's position to be too strong for an attack, he would endeavor to turn the Army of Tennessee's flank and threaten its rear. This would force Johnston to abandon his line and fall back to the next ridge, set up another defensive position, and hope that Sherman would come out and attack him. The terrain of central Georgia was, much to Sherman's chagrin, "one vast fort." The states high hills, ridges, ravines, dense underbrush and many streams made it the ideal scene for defensive war. Johnston did his best to use the terrain to his advantage.

29. *Baker Drunk* This entertaining scene of Baker intently playing a displaced piano amidst the flames of the burning house and the screams of shells helps substantiate the thought that Baker was drinking during the battle. Albert Castel, in his book, *Decision in the West: A History of the Atlanta Campaign*, states that Baker was actually taken out of command during the battle for being under the influence.

30. *Stewart's attack failed* The attack of Stewart's Division at Resaca on May 15th, can be counted as one of the great misfortunes of war. When Johnston gave General John B. Hood orders for his corps to begin the attack, Johnston felt that Hood would be hitting Sherman's exposed left flank. Hood ordered Stewart to carry out the attack. Stewart deployed his division in a double line of battle consisting of Gibson's and Clayton's Brigades on

the left and Stovall's and Baker's Brigades on the right.

As Stewart launched his attack, Johnston received word from General William H. T. Walker that the Federal right flank was crossing the Oostenaula River. Johnston sent word to Stewart to suspend his attack so that Johnston may look to the growing threat on his left flank. When Johnston's aide found Stewart and conveyed the message, the division was already engaged. To compound the problem, Union General Joseph Hooker, in the nick of time, bolstered his weak left flank with another division under Alpheus Williams. So, instead of hitting an exposed flank, Stewart's men ran head long into the waiting guns of Williams' men.

Besides having William's Division to worry about, Stewart ordered his division to execute a half whell to the left so as to bring his men to bear on, what he perceived to be, a weak Federal flank. The smoothness of the maneuver was hampered by dense thickets of undergrowth that threatened to break alignment. Undaunted, the Confederates continued on. The first of Stewart's brigades to come under fire were Clayton's men. Immediately, the veterans of that brigade realized that they were attacking an enemy in strength. The fire from the Federal line was devastating and twice, Clayton's men had to lie down for cover. The attack, though momentarily stalled, continued on. Clayton's men were able to push to within eighty yards of the Federal line until the fire was so destructive that they were forced to fall back. Next, Stovall's Georgia Brigade emerged from the undergrowth and was met by a huge volley of small arms and canister shot. Stunned, the brigade dissolved and men began running for the rear.

The Georgians passed through the ranks of Baker's advancing Alabama Brigade. The Alabamians marched through the thicket with their alignment becoming confused. Once out of the foliage, Baker's men fired a volley that achieved little success. After firing, they pushed on amidst the shot and shell to within, for some, thirty yards before it was all too much for them to take. Stewart, seeing that Baker's attack failed as well, called back the last brigade, Gibson's Louisianians, before it became too committed. In all, the attack cost Stewart approximately 1,000 men and what made the loss even more bitter was the fact that it shouldn't have even taken place.

31. *Troop Numbers* At the height of the campaign, Johnston's army was composed of three corps of infantry and one of cavalry. All told, it numbered 62,000 men. Sherman had three armies composed of 23 divisions. Sherman's total force numbered some 98,000 effectives.

32. *The Aborted Battle of Cassville* Johnston's battle plan in which he would assail the Federal Army at Cassville was a fine one and promised grand results. Johnston proposed at Adairsville, that the Army of Tennessee would separate forces in an attempt to get Sherman to do the same.Johnston ordered Hardee and most of his cavalry to march from Adairsville to Kingston, a town just seven miles west of Cassville. While Hardee marched to Kingston, Hood and Polk would march to Cassville. Johnston hoped that Sherman would divide his army and send troops in pursuit of the two Confederate columns. Once Sherman's men were behind them, Polk and Hood

would deploy and wait for Hardee to march the seven miles form Kingston. Together, the three corps would pounce on the Yankees following Hood and Polk. In such a fight, they would have good position, nearly even odds, and a resolve for success. Johnston's lieutenants eagerly accepted the proposal and set to work implementing it.

The plan worked, Union general McPhearson followed Hardee, while three corps under Hooker, Schofield, and Howard followed the advance of Polk and Hood. As planned, upon reaching Kingston, Hardee swung his corps east and linked up with Polk and Hood at Cassville. On the afternoon of the 18th of May, all was ready for the attack but Johnston chose to rest his tired army. On the 19th, Johnston was brought the good news that the three Federal corps were advancing into his trap. He ordered Hood forward down a road that would allow him to hit the Federal flank. As Hood executed the advance, he notice a column Federal troops but could not decide how large the force was or what type of troops they were. He only knew that the column threatened to attack his flank and rear. He sent word to Johnston of the new threat, and Johnston called Hood back.

The advancing column was, in actuality, just two divisions of Federal cavalry under McCook and Stoneman. It was these two divisions that were responsible for saving the three corps advancing into Johnston's trap.

The Confederates, now shaken, lost the initiative and Johnston ordered his corps commanders to take up a defensive position atop a ridge running south and east of Cassville. As the day progressed, Federal artillery opened fire on that position. The bombardment was heavy, and raked through Polk's Corps, holding the Confederate center, and Hood's men holding the right. The fire was so intense that Hood told Johnston that he could hold his position for no more than two hours and Polk said he could not hold for more than one.

33. *Axes* Sprott's statement advocating the use of axes is a perfect example of the mindset of both armies toward the use of breastworks. By the Spring of 1864, the soldiers had learned of the value of even hastily prepared defenses. In the attack, they knew that it was much harder to displace an enemy dug in behind works. On the defense, breastworks gave the men a sense of safety that strengthened their resolve to hold their position. The soldiers of the War Between the States were finally adapting tactics to match the rising use of rifled weaponry. By 1864, the Napoleonic strategy of massing firepower and carrying enemy positions through frontal assaults and the bayonet were considered foolhardy.

34. *Massed Battery* The artillery that fought so well at the Battle of New Hope Church was Eldridge's Artillery Battalion that consisted of Stanford's, Oliver's, and Fenner's Batteries.

35. *The Battle of New Hope Church* The Battle of New Hope Church, known as the "Hell Hole" by Federal soldiers, was a resounding Confederate victory. Major General A.P. Stewart's Division singlehandedly held off the attacks of three divisions of Federal General Joseph Hooker's XX Corps. Hooker had approximately 16,000 men attacking 4,000 under Stewart.

The brunt of the Confederate fire fell on Union General Alpheus William's front. Williams sent his division into the fight one brigade at a time. The Confederates, formed behind works, poured such an effective fire into William's brigades that each advance was sent reeling back. As the sun fell, Stewart's men raised a victorious "Rebel Yell" and the fight was over.

Stewart, in his official report, said of his casualties, "Our position was such that the enemy fire, which was very heavy, passed over the line to a great extent, which accounts for the fact that while so heavy a punishment was inflicted on the enemy, our own loss, between 300 and 400, was not greater." Stewart approximated enemy casualties at "3,000 to 5,000." Current sources put the number at approximately 700.

Stewart's full report can be found in the Official Records of the War of the Rebellion in Series I Volume XXXVIII.

36. *Cleburne at Pickett's Mill* At five p.m. on May 27th, 1864, Federal General Oliver O. Howard initiated an attack on what he believed to be a totally exposed Confederate right flank. Howard ordered one of his divisions, under Wood, to head the attack. Wood, in turn, ordered Brigadier General William B. Hazen forward.

Hazen's men moved out, through thick underbrush. The terrain reduced Hazen's neat ranks into a forward-moving mob. They emerged in a ravine and rushed to occupy an as yet unoccupied ridge. Just as they reached the base of the hill, Confederate Brigadier General Hiram Granbury's Texas Brigade of Cleburne's Division crested the top from the opposite side and opened fire. Hazen's men scrambled for cover and did their best to push Granbury off, but one unsupported brigade could not win the ridge. After forty minutes, the Federals, nearly out of ammunition, were forced to retreat.

Howard, upon Hazen's retreat, ordered the brigade of Gibson forward. Gibson's Brigade of Wood's Division fell to the same fate as Hazen's. Unsupported in their attack, Gibson too was forced to retreat. Then, at 6:30 p.m. Knefler's Brigade was sent forward to screen the rest of Howard's command while they built breastworks in a defensive position. Knefler's position in the underbrush was caught in a terrible enfilade fire from Granbury's Texans and he was pushed back a short distance where they threw up crude breastworks. Knefler's men were able to hold until the division had finished its works. At approximately 10:00 p.m., after removing the majority of Hazen's and Gibson's wounded, Knefler's Brigade was called back to the main line. No sooner had Knefler's men begun their retreat than Granbury's Confederates came racing down the ridge with a chilling "Rebel Yell." Granbury's counterattack, in the dark, sent the tired Federals reeling and many simply gave up.

With that effective assault, the Battle of Pickett's Mill was over. Cleburne placed enemy loss at 3,000 and his own at 448 men killed and wounded. Current sources have stated, however, that the Federal loss was 1,600. In either case, Cleburne had dealt Howard a decisive defeat.

37. *Kolbe's Farm* The action Sprott refers to was an engagement at Kolbe's Farm on June 22nd. The battle was fought by Federals in Hooker's XX Corps and elements of Major General John Schofield's Army of the Ohio.

Hood, thinking that the Federals were in column and on the march, planned a hasty attack that would assail the Federal left flank which had been perceived, by Hood, to be exposed. What Hood didn't know was that Hooker and Schofield's men were arrayed in line of battle. The brigades of Brown and Reynolds attacked north of the Powder Springs Road while the brigades of Cumming and Pettus attacked from the south side of the road.

The two assaulting columns advanced very close to the Federal lines before they were fired upon with a storm of small arms and artillery fire. Cumming's Brigade was set back by the volley of a single Federal Regiment, the 4th Kentucky.

Brown's and Reynold's Brigades were leveled by shell and canister rounds from five separate Federal batteries. When two brigades of Alpheus William's Federal division fired several quick volleys, the Confederates were sent running back to the safety of their own lines. This was fine revenge for Williams' Division that had taken such a beating at the Battle of New Hope Church.

When Stevenson's Confederates were repulsed, another division under Major General Thomas C. Hindman came into Federal view. The attacking Confederates fell under punishing Federal artillery fire and could not even reach the Union line. Hindman's men chose not to push the attack and the last assault fell away.

This impetuous attack by Hood cost his old corps 1,500 men killed and wounded. Federal casualties amounted to a slight 250 men. Brash attacks with little forethought would become Hood's awful trademark.

38. *The Battle of Peachtree Creek July 20th* Lieutenant General A. P. Stewart was actually grievously wounded at the Battle of Ezra Church on July 28th, 1864.

39. *Battle of Decatur* The fight described by Sprott, referred to as the Battle of Decatur by Confederate historians and the Battle of Atlanta by Union historians, was fought generally as Sprott describes it.

Confederate casualties have been approximated from 5,500-8,000 men. That late in the campaign and the war, the casualties were irreparable to the army and are evidence that Hood's offensive tactics were bleeding the army down. These casualties were even more disheartening when held in comparison to the Union numbers of killed and wounded that amounted to no more than 3,772. Among those Federals killed, however, was major General James B. McPhearson, commander of the Federal Army of the Tennessee. He was succeeded in command by Major General John A. Logan following the battle.

40. *The Battle of Ezra Church* Sprott refers to the battle fought on July 28th, 1864 as "the Battle of Peach tree Creek." It is understandable that Sprott might be confused as to dates and names of events in the Atlanta

Campaign; it is hard enough for historians to sort out details of that confusing Spring and summer. This bloody affair would prove to be the last action that the 40th Alabama would take part in before leaving the Army of Tennessee for guarding the coastal defenses in and around Mobile, Alabama.

Less than one week after the Battle of Decatur, Sherman began moving his army so as to take control of the last remaining Confederate railroad, Hood's sole supply line, the Macon and Western. Sherman moved the Army of the Tennessee from Bald Hill to just several miles west of Atlanta near a country chapel known as Ezra Church. Hood, once again as at Kolb Farm, sought to surprise the Army of the Tennessee and attack it while the Federals were on the march. To do this, he sent four divisions. Two of those divisions, Brown and Clayton, were commanded by Lieutenant General Stephen D. Lee and the other two, Walthall and Loring, were commanded by Lieutenant General A. P. Stewart.

The effectiveness of the attack hinged on the fact that the Federals, under O.O. Howard, would be caught completely unaware. When Lee attacked on the morning of the 28th, however, his troops found that the enemy was ready for them. The Federals had strengthened their position with works composed of dirt, logs, fence rails and pews from the church. Undeterred, Hood ordered three divisions into an attack that garnered nothing but additional casualties, including the critical wounding of Lieutenant General Stewart, who was felled by a mini ball that struck him in the head. In all, the Confederates lost approximately 3,000 men while Federal casualties amounted to just over 600.

In less than one week of fighting, Hood had lost more men than Joe Johnston had since the army left Dalton. From the Battle of Peachtree Creek to Ezra Church, Hood had sacrificed eleven thousand lives. In just the engagements of Peachtree Creek and Decatur, Hood lost 8,000.

41. Johnston Reappointed to Command Tennessee Army Although Davis' hostile attitude against Johnston had only grown worse since the unsuccessful Atlanta Campaign, General Robert E. Lee succeeded in persuading the president to reappoint him to command of the shattered Army of Tennessee. Johnston received word of Lee's support through one of his close friends in Richmond, Texas senator Louis T. Wigfall. Though Johnston had misgivings as to any political motive in his reappointment, Wigfall reassured him saying, "You are mistaken as to the motive which induced your being ordered to command. . . . It was out of kindness and real desire to obtain the benefit of your ability in this crisis. . . . It was Lee and not Davis. . . . For God's sake communicate with Lee fully and freely and with kindness and confidence and give him the full benefit of your judgement in this hour of peril."

This reassurance greatly affected General Johnston. He responded to Wigfall with a renewed sense of worth, declaring, "Be assured . . . that knight of old never fought under his King more loyally than I'll serve under General Lee." Johnston was officially reappointed to command, by Lee, on February 22nd, 1865.

42. *E.S. Gulley's Adventure* In his book, *Last Stand in the Carolinas: The Battle of Bentonville*, Mark Bradley provides a detailed account of this truly incredible accomplishment achieved by those men cut off behind Union lines following the attack Sprott mentions. The band of about seventy men were led by Colonel Anderson Searcy of the 45th Tennessee, Colonel E.S. Gulley of the 40th Alabama, Lieutenant Colonel Alexander Hall of the 45th Tennessee and Major William H. Joyner of the 18th Tennessee.

Assuming that they were surely to be captured, the group of Confederates were about to bury their weapons, lest they should fall into enemy hands, when a Federal soldier crawled out from underneath cover and surrendered to them. To the Confederate's amazement, other Federals in the immediate area followed suit until Searcy counted twelve prisoners. The group decided to attempt to steal around the right flank of the Federal army traveling by night and resting by day.

After nearly ten days and several near discoveries of their precarious position, the men were successful in returning to the army on March 28th. They were greeted with a hero's welcome. General John C. Brown called it the greatest campaign of any war and compared it to Napoleon's crossing the Alps.

43. *Ellerby's Death* Sergeant John H. Curry found Ellerby's body behind a log. He also found several other dead and wounded comrades of the 40th Alabama lying nearby, while endeavoring to find the regiment after fighting with the 54th Virginia Infantry for the majority of the day on March 19th.

44. *Johnston's Surrender to Sherman* Initially, the terms of surrender that Sherman offered to Johnston were generous. In light of Lincoln's assassination, the terms were more than a bitter Washington was willing to offer. Sherman was ordered to retract the initial terms and offer only what Grant had offered Lee. Under the terms of that surrender, the soldiers were permitted to return to their homes and await parole, officers were allowed to retain their side arms, and those soldiers who had them were permitted to keep their horses. Johnston, faced with the reopening of hostilities if he refused the surrender, accepted the terms and surrendered his entire department, numbering over 80,000 men, on April 26th, 1865. With this final formality the war had come to an end and the soldiers began the long trip home to rebuild their lives.

Bibliography

A manuscript of this scope deserves intensive scholarship to corroborate evidence. As an undergraduate participating in the annotation of this project, I was bound by constraints that kept me from giving the manuscript the attention that I felt it deserved. As a result of these constraints, I was relegated to conducting research through secondary source material. I utilized books that I believed most objectively covered the subject of my research and used them as guides to which I compared Sprott's accounts. If the two sources differed on any point I would research that incongruity until an answer was obtained. This system worked well under the circumstances.

Official Documents

The War of the Rebellion: A Compilation of the Official Records of the Union and Confederate Armies. Washington, D.C.: U.S. Government Printing Office, 1880-1901

Secondary Sources

Bradley, Mark L. *Last Stand in the Carolinas: The Battle of Bentonville.* Cambell, CA: Savas Woodbury Publishers, 1996.

Castel, Albert E. *Decision in the West: The Atlanta Campaign of 1864.* Lawrence, KS: University Press of Kansas, 1992.

Connelly, Thomas L. *Autumn of Glory: The Army of Tennessee 1862-1865.* Baton Rouge, LA: Louisiana State University Press, 1971.

Cozzens, Peter. *This Terrible Sound: The Battle of Chickamauga.* Chicago, IL: University of Illinois Press, 1992.

Cozzens, Peter. *The Shipwreck of Their Hopes: The Battles for Chattanooga.* Chicago, IL University of Illinois Press, 1994.

Daniels, Larry J. *Soldiering In the Army of Tennessee: A Portrait of Life in a Confederate Army.* Chapel Hill, N.C: University of North Carolina Press, 1991.

Griess, Thomas E., ed. *The West Point Military History Series: The American Civil War.* Wayne, N.J: Avery Publishing Group Inc., 1987.

The Editors of Time-Life Books. *Echoes of Glory: An Illustrated Atlas of the Civil War.* Alexandria, VA: Time-Life Books, 1991.

INDEX

A

Ackworth 108
Adairsville 96, 97, 163
Aiken 132
Alabama 3, 7, 13, 24, 28, 43, 48, 49,
59, 63, 72, 77, 78, 79, 83, 84, 86, 93,
94, 98, 112, 118, 122,131, 134, 137,
140
Alabama River 131
Alexander, T. F. 4, 13
Alexander's Bridge 46, 151
Allen, John A. 4
Allison, William S. 4, 13, 50, 104
Altman 40
Altman, W. A. 24, 25, 34, 40
Anderson 4, 25, 87, 168
Anderson, Buck 21, 25
Anderson, John 4, 13, 110
Armstrong, Hunter 25
Armstrong, W. C. 25
Artesia 19
Atlanta, GA 13, 14, 43, 81, 88, 89,
107, 117, 118, 119, 120, 122
Augle, Joshua 25
Augusta, GA 131, 144
Austin 98

B

Baines, S. R. 4
Baines, Sim 40
Baker 12, 63, 79, 86, 89, 92, 93, 94,
98, 102, 121, 122, 125, 134, 137, 138, 139
Baker, Alpheus 79, 144
Baker, Powell 81
Baker, R. H. 12
Baker, Rev. Joseph 12
Baker, W. H. 12
Baker's Creek 63
Ball, Sergeant 38
Banks, Jesse 4
Barker, B. S. 25
Barker, Hamp 25

Barr, Jimmie 51
Bate, Gen. 56
Bates 87
Battle of New Hope Church 13, 97,
106, 164, 166
Batton, William 25
Beauregard 37, 139
Beavers, A. E. 4
Bell, James 25
Benjamin, Judah P. 3
Benson, * 25
Bentonville10, 13, 14, 24, 27, 80, 81,
112, 136, 137, 139
Bevill, Bolivar 25
Big Black River 38
Bigbee River 19
Billups, John 4, 13
Bingham 112
Bingham, W. B. 11, 109
Birdsong's Ferry 37
Black's Bayou 31
Black's Bluff 8
Blackford 11
Blair 120
Blakely 123
Blakeney, Frank 9
Blakeney, Jack 25
Blount, R. P. 3
Blount, W. H 25
Bobbitt, * 25
Bobo 34
Bogan 19, 20
Bolling, John 4, 13
Bolling, Mark 4
"The Bonnie Blue Flag" 101
Boon, J. C. 4
Boon, S. D. 4, 13
Bragg 45, 48, 59, 66, 67, 70, 139
Bragg, Braxton 46, 154
Bragg, Gen. 37, 42, 43, 44, 45, 59,
67, 70, 73, 77, 120
Brandon, Miss. 41, 42, 60

Breckenridge 38, 41, 42, 56, 78, 87
Breckenridge, John C. 113
Breckinridge 41
Bridges, Maj. 32, 35
British America 2
Britt, J. A. J. 4, 13
Brooks, Wm. 4, 13, 121
Brown 29
Brown, A. R. 9, 11
Brown, Gov. 120
Brown, Robert A. 4
Brunson, Capt. 129
Brunson, T. M. 108
Brunson, Thomas M. 9, 11, 81, 108, 140
Bryan, B. 4
Buckalew, Ira 25
Buckner, Gen. 44
Buntin, William 95
Bunyard, Isham 4
Bunyard, John 4, 13, 52
Burns, Patrick 4
Burnt Bridge 90
Burnt Station 108
Bustain, Wm. 4, 14
Bustian 4, 123
Bustian, W. D. 123
Byron's Ford 47

C

Caesar 54
Calhoun 96
Camp Austill Marshall 12
Camp Forney 12, 13
Camp Timmons 28
Campbell, A. G. 8, 9, 81, 109
Campbell, Capt. 139
Canada 2
Canton, Miss. 16, 149
Cantonment 10, 12
Carroll, Joshua 25
Carrollton, Ala. 36
Cartersville 97
Cassville 97, 163
Century Magazine 109, 112

Chaney, Dr. 31
Charlotte, North Carolina 134
Chattahoochee River 117
Chattnooga, TN 42, 43, 44, 48, 51, 59, 66, 67, 68, 75, 87, 88, 107
Cheatham 53, 67, 70, 71, 74, 76, 78, 84, 87, 116, 119, 120, 132, 133
Cherokee 10
Chester 134
Chickamauga 13, 14, 42, 43, 45, 46, 47, 53, 54, 55, 56, 59, 60, 61, 72, 73, 74, 88, 110
Chickasaw Bayou 22, 28, 29, 147
Chickasaw Creek 28, 30
Childs, Miss 133
Choctaw County 8, 10, 12, 19, 20, 133
Cincinnati, OH 64, 153
Clayton 79, 86, 94, 98, 106, 136, 137
Cleburne 44, 54, 55, 70, 71, 75, 84, 87, 105, 113, 116, 119
Cobbs, Capt. 87
Cobbs, James 4, 11, 81
Cobbs, Jas. 9
Cole, W. G. 4
Coleman, A. A. 7, 12
Coleman, Capt. 72
Coleman, Col. 8
Coleman, Thos. W. 10, 19, 72
Colgin, Dr. George J. 12, 80, 81
Collier 109, 112
Colquit, Col. 50
Columbia, South Carolina 132, 133, 134
Columbus, Georgia 131
Columbus, Mississippi 19, 21
Commissary Department 130, 131, 135
Copeland, N. 25
Corinth 15, 19
Covington County 81
Craven House 66, 68
Crow Valley 86
Crowe C. C. 10, 81

Cuba, Ala. 8, 24, 35
Culpepper, A. 25
Culpepper, Ben 25
Culpepper, H. 25
Culpepper, Hubert 25
Culpepper, James 25
Culpepper, M 25
Culpepper, Mack 25
Culpepper, O. 25
Culpepper, Pet 25
Culpepper, Phillip 25
Cummings 12
Cunningham, T. R. 25
Curry, Rev. Jno. H. 62
Cusack, J. E. 25

D

Dallas County 12, 80
Dalton, Georgia 14, 27, 74, 75, 76, 78, 85, 89, 119, 120
Daniel, J. E. 4
Daniel, Ed. 4
Daniel, Seth 4
Daugherty, N. 5
Davidson, Joe 25
Davidson, W. R. 25
Davis, Mr. 48
Davis, President 65, 73, 120
Dawkins, J. T. 5
Dawkins, Jno. 50
Dawkins, John 13
Dean, Aleck 25
Dean, Alexander 27
Dearman, George 5
Dearman, Jas. 5
Dearman, N. B. 5, 13, 104
Deer Creek 31, 33, 36, 38
Demopolis, Ala. 7, 8, 9, 10, 14, 59, 66, 144
Dent, H. 3
Department of the Gulf 125
Dill, Sam 25
Dillard, Lieut Col. 50
"Dixie" 101
Dodson, Wesley 12, 25

Dog River 10
Dolive's Creek 123, 127
Donald, T. J. 5, 13
Donald, T. T. 5, 91
Donald, W. S. 5, 13
Donelson 3
Dougherty Bayou 34
Drummond, D. 5, 13
Dunn, James 13
Dunn, Jas 5

E

Eads, Robert 25, 27
Early, General 119
Ector 37, 38, 40, 43, 50, 53
Ector, Gen. 37, 47, 49, 50, 51, 52, 53, 56, 59, 60, 115
Ector's Texas Brigade 36, 115
Edward's Depot 38
Elder, Robert 25
Ellerbee, Adjutant 80, 81
Ellerbee, Clarence H. 9, 12, 80, 81, 109, 135, 138
Enterprise, Miss. 66
Evans, Sam 25
Everett, Henry 5, 13
Ezell, E. 5
Ezell, Elifus 50
Ezell, George 5
Ezell, P. 5

F

Falls 32
Faulkner, J. 5, 25
Faulkner, John D. 5, 77
Featherstone 31
Fergurson, Brigadier General 31
Ferrel, Bob 78
Ferrell, Robert 5
Fincher, H. S. 5, 13
Fincher, Hiram 121
Fish Lake 31, 32
Florida 12
Flowers, G. 5
Flowers, Goodman 52
Flowers, J. B. 25

165

Fluker, Eugene 5, 13
Ford, William 25
Forney, John H. 12
Forrest 50
Fort Gaines 122
Fort Jackson 29
Fort Morgan 122, 125
Fort Pemberton 35
Fort Warrenton 62, 63
Fowler 10
Franklin, H. 5
Freeman, John 25, 27
Freeman, S. 25
French 37, 114
French Broad River 134
French, Maj. Gen. 36, 59, 60
Friar's Point 34

G

Gantt, Capt. 112
Gantt, Hiram 11
Garrison, George 25
Garvin's Ferry 35, 40
Gaston 7, 8, 9, 20, 132
Gatewood, Ellis 25
Gatewood, Jas. 25
Georgia 42, 43, 44, 60, 79, 83, 107,
120, 121, 122, 124, 134, 137, 138,
144, 158, 160, 161, 162
Gibson 100, 121, 162, 165
Gilder, Pres. 94
Gist 36, 50
Glover, Wesley 25
Glover, Zeke 25
Going 109, 112
Goldsborough 137
Goldwaite, G. W. 7
Gooden, George 25
Gooden, Jas. 26
Graham, J. A. 5
Graniteville 132
Grant 34, 38, 85, 108, 147, 148,
149, 150, 154, 155, 157, 159, 169
Grant, Gen. 68, 85
Grant, Hiram 109

Green County 12, 82
Green, Col. 121
Green, Tom 111
Greenbacks 24
Greene, Andrew 5
Greene, Capt. 104
Greene, George 5
Greene, Isaiah 5
Greene, Tom 24
Greensboro, N.C. 136, 140, 145
Greenville 32
Greenwood 35, 36, 149
Grenada, Miss. 15
Greybacks 24
Grimes, J. D. 5, 14
Gulley 35
Gulley, Capt. 6, 7, 8, 17, 18, 35, 40
Gulley, Col. 60, 121, 122, 138
Gulley, E. S. 4, 7, 9, 11, 59, 61,
80, 140, 168
Gulley, Major 80

H

Hale, Jas. L. 25
Hales, J. O. 5, 14
Hall, Lieut. 139
Hall, W. P. 11, 109
Hall's Landing 123
Hall's Mill 7
Hamburg, S.C. 131, 132
Hamiter 10
Hammond, E. G. 5, 14, 50
Hammond, M. R. 5, 19
Hammond, W. B. 5
Hanna's Landing 34
Hardee 70, 74, 77, 84, 87, 89, 91,
97, 101, 102, 116, 119,120, 137, 139,
152, 156, 157, 159, 161, 163
Hardin, Hugh 26
Hardin, Joe 26
Hardin, Mad. 26
Harper, E. F. 5
Harris, H. C. 5, 14, 26
Harris, Henry 93
Harris, Henry C. 27

166

168

171

Z